"Planting acorns of hope, Anne Burnett provides a path of aspiration empowering parents raising their child—as well as themselves—into mighty oaks of strength and success. Here is a powerful story guiding parents and others toward accepting a child with autism, yet understanding what must be done in order for that individual to lead an aspiring, fulfilling and productive life."

—Stephen M. Shore, EdD
Assistant Professor of Special Education at Adelphi University
Board of Directors of the Autism Society
Internationally renowned educator and author on issues related to the
autism spectrum
www.autismasperger.net

"*Step Ahead of Autism* is an invaluable guide for anyone dealing with autism."

—T. Berry Brazelton, MD
Professor of Pediatrics Emeritus, Harvard Medical School and
Founder, Brazelton Touchpoints Center

"The exercises at the end of each chapter in *Step Ahead of Autism* speak directly to the parent—a novel and much needed approach toward building an effective partnership between parents and professionals."

—Catherine Freeman, MEd
Special Educator/Autism Consultant

STEP AHEAD OF
AUTISM

What *You* Can
Do to Ensure
the Best Possible
Outcome
for Your Child

Anne Moore Burnett

FOREWORD BY
T. Berry Brazelton, MD

39966 Grand Avenue
North Branch, MN 55056
Phone: 651-277-1400 or 800-895-4585
Fax: 651-277-1203
www.sunriseriverpress.com

Edit by Karen Chernyaev
Layout by Monica Seiberlich
Cover design by Connie DeFlorin

ISBN 978-1-934716-25-0
Item No. SRP625

Library of Congress Cataloging-in-Publication Data

Burnett, Anne Moore.
  Step ahead of autism : what you can do to ensure the best possible outcome for your child / by Anne Moore Burnett.
    p. cm.
  Includes bibliographical references and index.
  ISBN 978-1-934716-25-0
  1. Autistic children--Popular works. 2. Autism--Popular works. I. Title.
  RJ506.A9B873 2011
  618.92'85882--dc23
                          2011026125

Printed in USA

10 9 8 7 6 5 4 3 2 1

Dedication

For my children, Joey and Mattie

Contents

Foreword

I first met Anne Burnett and her son Joey eighteen years ago, when Joey was just under two and a half. Anne entered my office at Boston Children's Hospital Developmental Center with a notebook filled with copious notes about Joey's unusual behaviors and sensitivities. I was impressed by her early recognition of Joey's autistic-like symptoms but even more by her ability to quickly determine that she needed to draw from her own strength and courage and become the true authority on her child—the authority that every autistic child needs his or her parent to be.

According to the Centers for Disease Control and Prevention, the prevalence of autism has risen to 1 in every 110 births in the United States and 1 in 70 boys. Autism continues to rise at an average rate of 10–17 percent per year.[1] *Step Ahead of Autism* focuses on the parents and caregivers of the autistic child. It instructs and guides them about how to react so they can reach their difficult child.

Step Ahead of Autism can inspire and empower parents by teaching them how to make sound decisions for and about their autistic children. The book, moving and beautifully written, takes you through Anne's journey and shows you in detail how you, as a parent, can successfully guide your child. At the end of each chapter, *Step Ahead of Autism* provides you with the tools, strategies, and worksheets you need to provide your child with a positive outcome.

Doctors, psychologists, counselors, and educators have referred hundreds of parents to Anne Burnett over the past eighteen years. She has helped these hundreds of parents by sharing how she supported Joey and by helping them observe, advocate for, and support their children. She shares her philosophy with parents who are battling several issues or just one. Anne's success story—taking Joey from the diagnosis of severe pervasive developmental disorder to his becoming a thriving, social, articulate young man at Brown University—proves every parent's innate ability to look deep within and to courageously lead his or her child to a future full of hope and promise.

Parents are aware of the importance of early diagnosis. *Step Ahead of Autism* not only shows you how to better inform your pediatrician of your concerns about your child's behavior, but it continues to provide you with guidance every step of the way in raising a child through—and beyond—the autism diagnosis.

I am proud to be a part of Joey's success. He is now a junior at Brown. Anne and he deserve a great deal of credit. Joey's story instructs us what is possible when you, as a parent, arm yourself with powerful information, observe your child, trust your instincts, and advocate for what your child needs. *Step Ahead of Autism* will help you create what's possible for your child—whatever that future is.

T. Berry Brazelton, MD
Professor of Pediatrics Emeritus, Harvard Medical School
Founder, Brazelton Touchpoints Center

Acknowledgments

Thanks to all of you who helped make the completion of this marathon possible. Without you, I would have never crossed the finish line.

A heartfelt thanks to my son Joey for your honesty, openness, and keen insight into this project and into your life; and to my son Mattie for your incredible patience, sensitivity, and sense of humor about my hours spent on this project. I am truly blessed.

To my other family members: to Joe, Bob, Mary, Kathy, and Libby for giving your baby sister the motivation, encouragement, love, and support to keep on running. To my late mom, for passing on your maternal gifts. To my late dad for teaching me to always look at how far I've come, not how long the journey is.

To my dear friends: Margaret Spinale for her positive e-mails and power talks, and her daughter, Deanna, for sharing her personal experiences. To Karla for her motivating messages and inspiring runs. To Pam for her morning phone calls, making me laugh and reminding me to take breaks. Thank you all for still being on the other end of the phone and a part of my life.

To Lady, Brady, and Yuki for keeping me company.

Thanks to Sippican Lands Trust for giving me the time to complete this project. To Michelle and Jonathan Pope, proprietors of Uncle Jon's Café, for providing a soothing spot to write, and to their staff for always making sure my coffee was steaming hot. Thanks to Ted and Pete for giving me space when I needed it and providing encouragement when I didn't.

Thanks to the staff and educators at Sippican Elementary School, Project Grow, Friends Academy, and Bishop Stang High School for providing Joey with a nurturing education and for enriching our lives.

I extend my gratitude to T. Berry Brazelton, MD; Karen Levine, PhD; Susan Christian, RN; Cathy Freeman, autism specialist; and Deanna Feroli for your contributions.

To my agent, Jeanne Fredericks, for helping me understand what I didn't know and staying committed to this project.

A special thanks to Lisa Tener, my editor, teacher, guide, and friend—this project would have never happened without you, and for that I am truly indebted; and thank-you to my classmates in Lisa's Bring Your Book to Life program for your insightful feedback and inspiration.

Preface

In 1992 my son Joey was diagnosed at the severe end of the autism spectrum, with an array of disorders and deficits in social interaction, speech, behaviors, and responses to sensory experiences. At three years old he didn't speak but screeched and squealed to get his needs met. Today he is a junior at Brown University—not through a miracle cure but through a ten-step system I've developed to "beat" the diagnosis of autism.

Autism, uncommon in 1990, began to soar in 1995. In the ten years between 1995 and 2005, the number of U.S. schoolchildren with autism diagnoses increased by more than 800 percent. In 1991 the Autism Diagnostic Interview, the first generally recognized tool for diagnosing autism, was released. In 1994 the American Psychiatric Association published the fourth edition of the *Diagnostic and Statistical Manual (DSM-IV)*, which refined diagnostic criteria for autistic disorder. Autism became a spectrum disorder; in essence, it became possible for someone to be diagnosed as very autistic or mildly autistic. Autism had never been tracked as an educational statistic before 1990. Since 1990 the incidence of autism in schools has risen consistently.

The Centers for Disease Control and Prevention states in its 2009 findings that autism is more prevalent than cancer, cerebral palsy, Down syndrome, hearing loss, and vision impairment in children ages eighteen and under and is just as common as juvenile diabetes.[2] Suspecting that your child has a learning disorder is frightening. Hearing a confirmed diagnosis is alarming at best. In some ways, Joey's diagnosis should not have surprised me. I'd been documenting his behavior for two years. In other ways, I felt completely numb by the finality of "autism."

Most parents, when they first hear a spectrum disorder diagnosis, find themselves in the same place I was—stuck, unable to move forward. Even with the help of a trusted pediatrician, parents are often left with sinking feelings of powerlessness, helplessness, and confusion. I wrote this book to share my story, yes, but to share so much more. I want to give you—a person touched by autism—a place to feel safe and validated in the feelings you are experiencing today and to teach you tips and strategies that empower you for the challenges you will face tomorrow.

These days, bookstore shelves are well stocked with helpful books about autism and the other spectrum disorders. Research studies occur regularly and have increased at a rate of 15 percent per year. But little information is available to empower and support parents in the personal growth they will be required to make to successfully raise a happy, healthy, autistic child into a confident adult.

In her book *The Way I See It*, Temple Grandin, PhD, diagnosed as autistic, offers her wisdom and personal reflections on autism and shares her perspective on teaching, behavior, work, and the adult life of people with autism. The following quote, taken from her book, supports my belief that we as caretakers can make a difference:

> My life and career could have been derailed and wrecked if my mother and business associates had not pushed me to do things. . . . The best thing a parent can do for their newly diagnosed child is to watch and learn how their child functions, acts, and reacts to his or her world.

Parenting a healthy child is demanding. Raising an autistic child requires stepping up to an even greater challenge. To raise your child to be the best he can be, you as parent need support and guidance. My ability to navigate the ups and downs of autism led me to confront many unfounded beliefs, in well-meaning people, that hinder autistic children from living their best. My commitment to my son guided me on an eighteen-year journey to uncover concepts, techniques, and practices that worked for me and that I began sharing with other parents and now share with you in *Step Ahead of Autism*.

This book is part story, part how-to, and part advocacy. It's meant to touch hearts, to educate, and to ensure that early diagnosis and intervention are the primary goals of every parent, pediatrician, educator, and caregiver. It provides you with a guide so you can recognize, embrace, and defeat autism. Doctors, counselors, educators, day care workers, and teaching assistants—anyone associated with an autistic child—will benefit from reading *Step Ahead of Autism*.

Step Ahead to a Better Outcome

Wisdom becomes knowledge when it is personal experience.
—Yogi Bhajan

I looked in the mirror, taking inventory one last time, comforted that my earrings now matched. Graduation day had finally arrived, bringing with it a perfect summer day in early June. The forecast—82 degrees, clear and sunny skies—made me glad the New England weatherman had been right. Everything else arranged, my youngest son, Mattie, at last found a sports jacket to wear. At eleven years old, he was 5 feet 10 and wore size 11 men's shoes, so finding dress attire that fit him, without breaking the bank, provided a challenge. Luckily, his dad had mustered up a navy blue Anderson-Little brass-buttoned coat that oddly enough still looked in style. Despite my son's displeasure with another hand-me-down and sleeves that reached the base of his thumbs, I don't think I ever remember Mattie looking more handsome than he did that day. For myself, I found a crepe pink suit that flowed and ebbed at just the right angles on my waist, kindly camouflaging the excess weight I had accumulated over the past few months snacking nervously on cheddar cheese popcorn while awaiting word on Joey's acceptance to Brown University—not to mention the cold champagne and celebratory chocolate fudge cheesecake when we finally heard.

We planned to hold a graduation party following the ceremony at a social hall about a block away from our home. More than one hundred years old, the hall sits on the edge of the harbor, the view as picturesque as the ocean itself. In early spring, sailboats of all sizes, shapes, and colors had begun daubing the water as an artist would stroke his canvas, and as summer grew close, the paint-by-number seascape seemed almost complete. We had invited everyone to the party—our family, friends, Joey's friends, doctors, teachers—everyone who knew Joey. My nieces planned to head to the hall first thing that morning to put up easels and photo boards of Joey, displaying his progress throughout the years. So Mattie wouldn't feel left out, I made up two boards depicting how far he had come, even though he was six and a half years younger than Joey and had issues of a different color.

We filed into our reserved seats. Danny, my ex-husband and Joey's dad, sat at my left, and Mattie sat at my right, his sweaty hand squished in mine. Or was mine squished in his? The heat of the auditorium, coupled with the excitement of the day, warmed us all, temporarily pasting us back together as a family. For a moment I almost forgot I was divorced.

"Pomp and Circumstance" brought us eagerly to our feet, and the graduates marched in. Catching sight of the valedictorian, a handsome young man a step ahead of the pack, I trembled. For a brief moment I couldn't breathe. I squeezed Mattie's hand a little tighter; he handed me a Kleenex after he fetched one for himself. Poised, the young man continued down the aisle, climbed up to the podium, and began to speak. Words poured from his lips, effortlessly, as if he had done this a thousand times before. His message, as moving and powerful as the entrance music itself, left his captivated audience wondering when the music had ended and his speech had begun. Upon his conclusion, thunderous applause filled every crevice of the hall. Families and fellow students stood tall in approval as Joey, my son, my valedictorian, made his way back to his seat. The three of us sat there stuck together, sobbing, sniffling, and shaking in unison. Eventually we pulled ourselves apart and forced our focus on the third speaker, as the second one had already passed us by.

As the other speakers took their turns at the podium, my mind wandered back fifteen years. Fifteen years earlier, I was you—standing in a bookstore, perusing the library, desperately seeking some scrap of information to help me understand what was going on with my child. My son

Joey had been diagnosed at age two with a severe pervasive developmental disorder (PDD), a neurological disorder in the autism spectrum.

Joey had no form of speech except for frustrated high-pitched squeals. He flapped his arms, swung in his chair for hours, slept and ate poorly, didn't like to snuggle, and easily startled. He was tactile defensive, obsessed about certain toys, and hated candles, the sensation he felt when the car slowed down, sand, smells, noise, being touched—the list went on. Numerous doctors, including noted pediatrician T. Berry Brazelton, had diagnosed Joey. Dr. Brazelton and his team recommended that Joey attend the May Institute, a year-round, residential-only program for acutely autistic and mentally challenged children.

My husband, who's about as straightforward as they come, asked Dr. Brazelton if he thought Joey would ever talk. Dr. Brazelton replied in shades of gray: "They are making great strides at the May, and that would be Joey's best hope." I felt as if I lost my husband that day. No, he didn't pass away; he is very much alive. I felt I lost my husband to the bleak forecasts issued by most of the doctors we saw.

Autism is not a disease; it is a disturbance in psychological development. Doctors can make an educated, experienced best guess at an autistic child's outcome, but as my story—and those of other parents—will show you, and as Dr. Brazelton implied, doctors can't really know.

What doctors do know is that autism occurs more often than Down syndrome, at a rate of 1 in 110 births and climbing. They know that the earlier the diagnosis and the earlier the intervention of services, the better the outcome.[3] Denial, anger, and confusion are normal reactions to learning that your child has been diagnosed with a developmental disorder. Your choice as a parent is to wallow in the "why me's," the denial, and the anger or to accept, adapt, and advocate. You can turn the denial into determination, the anger into energy, and the "why me's" into "watch me." I know. I did, and I will show you how to do the same.

Step Ahead of Autism cuts through the mounds of information available to parents on what is needed to raise an autistic child and provides clear, concise steps you can take now to provide your child with his or her best outcome. You will hear from Joey's doctors and educators on how the steps I and other parents have taken greatly impacted the positive results for our children.

Autism is not a puzzle but an opportunity to step up to the challenge and be the best parent you can be. Before you can transform your autistic child, you have to transform yourself, and this book will help you. It is time to leave the "Why does autism occur?" to the researchers and to move forward. Fifteen years ago, I felt powerless, helpless, overwhelmed, and confused. I also felt very much alone and that I had done something wrong as a first-time mother. If I had known then what I know now, I would have saved myself and others a lot of grief and agony. There is help. There are solutions. You can learn how to make a positive difference in your and your autistic child's life.

In the following chapters, I will help you learn to practice ten steps in any situation: trust, observe, accept, adapt, ascertain, assess your attitude, advocate, assert your authority, delegate, and aspire. As you read through the steps, begin to implement the key words into your daily life. Post them on your fridge, put them on your computer as a screen saver, or attach them to your child's car seat—anywhere they will empower and remind you to lay the foundation for your child's success through the daily practice of these steps.

I designed the steps knowing that most parents feel overwhelmed and have lengthy to-do lists. In my courses and teleseminars, which bring you the latest learning about and approaches to autism, so that you can be the parent your child needs, parents read through one chapter and apply the corresponding step each week. You may want to use this book similarly, applying one step (one chapter) per week to give yourself time to acclimate to each step.

On June 1, 2008, Joey became valedictorian of his high school senior class and the following fall became a freshman at Brown University. He is a bright, happy, and socially and emotionally adjusted young man with friends and peers alike. Rather than focus on the changes in him that created such an outcome, I point to the changes I had to make—the ways I had to grow, the skills I needed to develop, the innate abilities I needed to trust—to support this unusual outcome. How we choose to parent an autistic child makes a difference. It did to Joey.

The Ten Steps

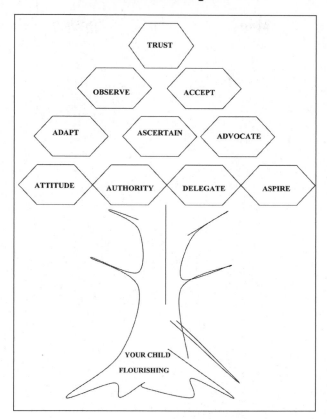

TRUST
Hopeful reliance on what will happen in
the future

OBSERVE
To watch somebody attentively

ACCEPT
To acknowledge a fact or truth and come
to terms with it

ADAPT
To put oneself in harmony with changed
circumstances

ASCERTAIN
To find out something with certainty; to
learn and discover

ADVOCATE
To plead in favor of

Assess Your
ATTITUDE
An opinion or general feeling about
something

Assert Your
AUTHORITY
To state or declare positively and often
forcefully or aggressively that you are
the person in command

DELEGATE
To give somebody else the power to act
and make decisions on your behalf

ASPIRE
To seek to attain or accomplish a particular goal; ascend, soar

Step One:
TRUST

/Trust/ **Hopeful reliance on what will happen in the future**

The vivid August sun gleamed down through the Mazda's small sunroof onto the front passenger seat, orchestrating a rectangular-shaped light show on my capris. My husband, Danny, was behind the wheel. I closed my eyes, my fingers tapping out the words to Van Morrison's "Moondance" in rhythm with the radio. I thought about the current connection of our lives. Danny and I both held substantial positions in the financial world; he a top mortgage broker with a large firm, and I the first woman inducted into a senior management position with Randolph Savings Bank since its inception in 1851.

Married seven years, we had let our advancing careers define our lives. We spent most of our time together talking work strategies and office politics. It left me feeling almost single and as if our only other bond was our checking account.

Our typical summer getaway meant spending a night at one of our preferred settings, the Red Jacket Beach Resort in South Yarmouth, Massachusetts. The resort, situated on a breathtaking sweep of private ocean beach, offered indoor and outdoor pools, two restaurants, and—most importantly—waitstaff who served you no matter where you lounged, making the resort our crown choice for collapsing in a chair with a good book or watching the waves play tag while sipping on drinks. The atmosphere made me feel a million miles away from our house, even though we were only forty-five minutes from Wareham.

Akin to skilled hunters, we tracked down two empty chairs on the beach—strategically placed between the flock of waitpeople and the towel shed—and made camp. We ordered our drinks—a tall whiskey sour with plenty of ice for Danny and a pinot grigio for me. After chatting about work for our normal ten- to fifteen-minute allotment, we settled into our own routines. Danny stretched out for a nap under his homemade sun umbrella, the most recent copy of *Banker and Tradesman*, while I soaked in the sun and watched people, wondering what Danny and I would talk about if we didn't have work in common.

A flying plastic blue beach shovel interrupted my thoughts, landing, sand first, in my lap. Startled, I jumped up, brushed myself off, and looked up to find a little boy with brown eyes and wavy white blond hair wearing nothing but a Sesame Street diaper and the remnants of what appeared to be a grape Popsicle on his face. The boy picked up the shovel and began patting my stomach, tossing sand in all directions. His father, equally as palatable, ran over, picked him up in the air, and twirled him around. The little boy let out a deep belly laugh, so loud it made me laugh, and the proud but embarrassed father apologized for his son's messy intrusion.

"No problem," I said, "he's adorable. How old is he?"

"Fifteen months," the boy's father replied as he looked around. "And what's your secret?"

"Excuse me?"

"How are you able to get a moment's peace? Where are your little monsters hiding?"

"I, I mean we (signaling to Danny, who now snored so profusely that his umbrella set sail) don't have any children, yet . . . but I . . . we . . . can't wait."

"Don't wait too long. They're hard to keep up with."

I tickled the little boy's belly while the father held him high, and off they went, laughing and chasing each other, kicking up sand in their wake. Watching them run away down the beach, for the first time in a long time I felt barren and painfully empty. I wanted them to come back so I could pretend they were mine and that we were a family and that the past four and a half years of waiting while munching fertility pills had been a bad dream. Just then the waitress came by, clanging ice cubes and shouting out for drink requests, and Danny woke up.

"What are you looking at?" he asked, still half-asleep.

"Nothing . . . really. I just thought I saw someone I knew." I sat back down.

Over the weekend, I continued to see the father–son duo by the pool, in restaurants, and on the beach. I even found myself taking walks by the children's playground in hopes of a glimpse. Somehow seeing them gave me comfort and made the time until Danny and I would be parents seem much closer than we had been told. In April our social worker had instructed us to check back with her in January of the following year to see where we were on the list for adoption. I hardly paid attention to her instructions anymore. We were initially told the entire adoption process would take a year and a half. Four and a half years later, I no longer allowed myself to think it would ever happen. But that day, filling the desolate gorge in my heart with thoughts of my next career move or what to wear to Friday night's social engagement failed, giving permission to that distant yearning for precious life to seep back in and run sharply through my veins. I suddenly felt cold on this 92-degree summer day.

As we checked out of our room, I saw the little boy one last time, clinging to his dad's legs at the front desk. I walked over, bent down, and tickled his belly until his addictive laughter rang through the lobby. He extended his little hand out to hold mine. With his dad's eyes granting me permission, I held the little boy's fingers, giving them a gentle squeeze. In that instant, something deep inside me bloomed. Our time as parents had come—I could feel it.

On the way home, I told Danny about the little boy and the message his presence had sent to me. Danny tried to comfort me, worried that my hopes would deflate, since we'd been told that adoption would be at least five months away. I told him I agreed and convincingly dismissed the feeling as a fleeting maternal moment, but I planned to call our social worker the minute I got to work on Monday.

The next day I poured myself a cup of coffee, made the normal Monday morning salutations to members of my staff, and excused myself for an early morning conference call. I closed the glass-paned door to my office—trying to get some morsel of privacy—and dialed the number of my social worker, Elaine. I could barely contain myself as the secretary put me through to Elaine.

"Elaine speaking."

"Hi, Elaine, it's Anne Burnett. How are you?"

"Good, Anne . . . and you?"

"Good. I know I'm not supposed to call until January, but the strangest thing happened and, well, my instinct told me to call."

"You must have ESP. I planned to call you at 9:30 this morning . . . I just wanted to give you time to get settled in and pour yourself some coffee."

"I have my coffee."

"And I have a beautiful baby boy for you. Congratulations, you're a mom!"

Your Exercise

I don't have ESP or possess a sixth sense, I can assure you. But I felt an unexplained connection to the little boy. I had never seen him or his father before. I had been to the Red Jacket many times over the years and had witnessed many children playing with their parents. Though the little boy had no knowledge of me or my situation, I strangely felt a connection back from him—a feeling in my gut.

When raising a child, parents are called upon to make decisions—from rules about diet to discipline to dating. When raising an autistic child, you will be faced with additional, and difficult, layers of decisions, including decisions about therapies, special diets, and school programs. In addition, your child might not be capable of contributing to the decision-making process due to his or her inability to communicate. These decisions create a lot of pressure, as they will greatly influence your child's outcome. Your ability to decide—and to trust in your decision—is paramount.

Parents, I believe, are naturally blessed with an innate sense—a mother's intuition, if you will. Not until my intuition was continually tested by the major choices I had to make for Joey, did I begin to question myself. I realized that I needed to continually develop trust in myself and nurture my intuition or it would wither, and I would lose focus on what needed to be done and my confidence in what I was doing.

Your intuition, sometimes referred to as your inner guidance, is a mechanism of inner or instinctive knowing that neither requires nor employs logical thought processes. It is an alternative source of knowledge, a level of awareness, or an inner voice. We all possess this mechanism to varying degrees, as well as the capacity to develop it further.

Intuition is something we all have, yet many of us are hesitant to believe in, use, or trust it. How many times have you had that feeling in your stomach compelling you to do, or not do, something for no apparent reason? Listening to it might have helped you avoid a traffic accident, be at the right place at the right time for getting that great job, or meet that special person. However, we can trust our intuition only as much as we trust ourselves. As we go through life, we tend to get more and more out of touch with our inner selves and our own truth, until we end up living a life that feels too much like work. We get out of touch with who we really are and what's right for us and go farther and farther off our own unique paths. We fall into a trap of reacting to life and coping with what happens instead of actively creating a life that's right for us. We lose our way because we don't recognize how important it is to trust ourselves.

Tips

- *Quiet your mind and listen.* Take time each day to experience silence. Practice calming your mind by using whatever breathing or meditative technique you prefer. Let go of the inclination to think, analyze, and try to know everything. Be open and listen.
- *Pay attention and be aware.* To increase your intuitive abilities, you must pay attention to what is going on around you.
- *Reflect at the end of the day.* Before you go to bed at night, reflect upon questions and issues for which you couldn't find solutions during the day. Think about and explore different possibilities. This will trigger your imagination and put your subconscious to work at furnishing you with creative solutions while you sleep.
- *Journal.* When you take time to write or journal, you tap into thoughts, feelings, and ideas you're not typically conscious of. This is an excellent way to release inner messages, insights, or hidden knowledge about a situation or problem that requires solving.

Exercise

Write down a question you are searching for an answer to. Make the issue specific to your life and something that you ultimately could resolve on your own, not something you have no control over. Example: "Should I enroll my autistic child in swimming classes?"

_____

_____

_____

_____

Being completely honest with yourself about how you feel, write down what you truly hope the best resolution would be and why. Example: "I think it would help relieve some of my child's anxiety and hyperactivity."

_____

_____

_____

_____

Why? _____

_____

_____

_____

Bringing all your issues into the light of awareness around your question, write down why you don't trust that your answer is the right one. Example: "I'm concerned the instructor might not have the patience required to teach my son."

_____

_____

_____

_____

Write down reasons you hope your answer is the correct one. Example: "If my son relaxed more, I think he would be happier and less aggressive."

_____

_____

_____

Now walk away from this exercise. Before you go to sleep tonight, think about your question and your answers. When you wake up, write down your first thoughts. Chances are more than likely that you will have your answer. If not, repeat this exercise. Self-trust takes practice and requires you to believe in yourself. Being aware of the feelings you are holding in your body and connecting more fully with your inner wisdom gives you permission to choose. Rather than simply reacting to events around you, be proactive in creating your life.

Your inner voice, your inner guide, is a gift to nurture and cherish. Every decision you make in opposition to your own inner wisdom is destined to fail in one way or another. Trusting yourself defines your destiny and leads you down the path you are meant to follow.

Step Two:
OBSERVE

/Observe/ **To watch somebody attentively**

We drove down the rocky coastal road to the foster parents' home, both of us frozen silent in anticipation. Chilled, I pressed my face against the sun-drenched window and recalled the launch of this journey four and a half years before. A sea of home studies, family histories, medical reports, college transcripts, and personal recommendations drifted by, the culmination granting us passage to today's voyage. It's funny: Anyone can get pregnant. You don't need a job, a home, a college degree, or even a high school diploma. But when you adopt, the interrogation lights go up and the self-advocating begins. Drained by this laborious process, our relationship emotionally shipwrecked, my husband and I clung to the prospect of smooth seas ahead.

An hour later, we stood inside the vestibule of Joey's foster parents' home. Joey—five weeks old; brown eyes, brown hair, 7 pounds 9 ounces—possessed ten fingers, ten toes, and all the additional attributes a healthy, beloved baby boy could hold. With years of constructing a paternal shelter now concluded, Danny anxiously cupped his new son to his chest, housing them both. Foreign to this novel refuge, Joey cried in distress, abruptly severing their fusion. Danny hastily handed Joey back to the foster mom, secretly relieved that Joey's anguish did not cease upon transfer. The disheveled woman, unfettered, gently comforted Danny, "Hopefully Joey will find contentment in his new home." Hopefully? What a pessimistic point of view. Clearly, her grief around Joey's departure had affected her word choice.

The ride back home eludes me, as sheer joy navigated my judgment and actions for the remainder of the day. The next four nights, however, I do remember: Joey never ever slept. Not only did he not sleep, he didn't like being awake. He would stretch out his body tightly and stiffly, fending off anyone from touching him. We tried everything: music, massage, rocking, warm baths—even placing his infant seat on top of the clothes dryer while I ran a load of laundry, praying the vibration would lull him to sleep. Finally, after four nights of torture, I called the foster mom. Did Joey have colic? Did he exhibit this level of distress with her? What could I do to calm him? Standing in Joey's room, Joey shrieking in the background, I grasped for any guidance she could give me.

"We took him three times to the doctor. He's not colicky." The phone went silent. The indifference in her voice confirmed my suspicion that something was wrong. Yet what did I know, me, a mother of five days?

Joey didn't sleep through the night until seventeen months of age.

We continued to note an array of subtleties, from Joey's poor and particular appetite to his high sensitivity to sounds and smells. I mentioned these and other "quirks" during every visit to the pediatrician's office during those first two years. Joey's doctor, a mother of five, quickly dismissed my concerns as maternal inexperience. The visits left me feeling foolish and inferior. I found myself questioning my abilities as a mother.

Then, one night at my sister's house for dinner, I experienced another confirmation. My sister Libby, fourteen months my elder and the mother of ten children, took it upon herself to coddle Joey when his nightly routine of crying, stiffening, and withdrawal commenced. Sure that she had experienced these symptoms with one of her own, she optimistically whisked him off to the den to rock him with his bottle. Five minutes later, Libby appeared, her face strained and concerned. "It's definitely not colic or gas; you're right." She anxiously placed Joey back in my lap.

From that moment on, I kept a log of what I witnessed as "odd" behavior. Thriving on routine at six months, hand flapping at nine months, lining up toys at ten months, and no language. No gurgling, no cooing—

nothing except screeches and squeals. I included dates, times, locations, and all concerning behaviors. Soon I accumulated enough information to warrant another trip to the pediatrician's office.

With Joey now 2.3 years old and only a month since we had last seen the doctor, I armed myself with the updated log of his behavior. The office had three pediatricians, all women, the eldest Joey's doctor. The youngest doctor I didn't know. My sister recommended that I make an appointment with the middle one, Dr. Sharon Shaw. The size of the office made it difficult for me to bypass Joey's original doctor without feeling disloyal. At the same time, I needed someone who would seriously listen to my story and look at my log, even though the majority of Joey's odd behavior seemed incredibly subtle.

Not five minutes into my dissertation, Dr. Shaw excused herself from the room. Within seconds, Sue, everyone's favorite nurse, came in and handed me a piece of paper. I couldn't make out the doctor's writing. Below some scribbled name it said, "Boston Children's Hospital." I looked at her, confused. She said, "Go home. I'll call the doctor for you and set up the appointment. I'll get back to you within the hour."

I had a thousand questions but did as I was told, methodically, as if someone had pulled me out the door. On the way home, I feverishly went over the log in my head—the subtleties, the quirks, the day we brought Joey home—frantically trying to piece together the picture Dr. Shaw must have seen. Then it hit me: She thinks Joey is autistic. I had seen some of the subtle behaviors Joey was exibiting before, in a five-year-old-girl named Angela who moved into the home next to my parents' when I was fourteen. Angela, nonverbal, displayed repetitive behaviors continuously throughout the day. I remember one morning when I was at her home, Angela spent three hours attempting to cross over the threshold into the kitchen where I was talking to her mom, Diane—each attempt increasing Angela's and Diane's frustration. "It drives me crazy she gets so worked up trying to go from room to room," said Diane.

"She's trying to repeat, exactly, step for step, what she did before."

Diane looked at me puzzled.

"I'm guessing that's what she is doing." To this day, I don't know why I thought that—I sensed it.

From then on, I became Angela's babysitter and went with her and her mom to doctor visits and helped with patterning. Patterning involved

A Nurse's Perspective

Typically, the first person you talk with when you go to the pediatrician's office is a nurse. Nurses usually take a history and briefly list your concerns for the doctor. It is of great benefit to the nurse and doctor if you arrive for your visit with a written list of concerns. The clearer and more concise you make the list, the better. Use bullets or highlighting to indicate behaviors or mannerisms that you find most troubling.

Never feel like any question is silly, and never worry that you will take up too much of the doctor's or nurse's time. If any aspect of your child's behavior troubles you, mention it, and be sure to make it clear that you feel it is a problem. Don't be vague in expressing issues. You want to be sure the doctor realizes that this is an area of real concern for you and your child.

I suggest you create a timeline of behaviors with dates and take it with you to the visit. Note when each behavior began and how long it lasted, because some behaviors can disappear and be replaced by others. A timeline

- allows you to accurately answer the doctor's questions about when each behavior started;
- serves as a framework for you to build upon as time goes on;
- makes intakes easier in the event your child is referred for multiple evaluations with specialists, speech therapists, and other providers, who will ask you the same questions over and over again;
- saves you from having to remember dates and details during an office visit, when you might be feeling overwhelmed or might be distracted if your child becomes impatient or uncooperative.

Pediatricians and nurses always have the best interests of your child at heart, but remember that an office visit provides only a brief snapshot of your child. Sometimes it can be difficult for doctors and nurses to decipher whether what they observe is typical. Your child might appear shy or anxious in the office setting and might not demonstrate the behaviors that concern you in front of the doctor. Doctors and nurses rely heavily upon you to report what you observe at home. No one knows your child as well as you do. Trust your instincts and always advocate strongly for your child. You do know best.

Susan Christian, RN
Nurse Manager
Bramblebush Pediatrics

Angela lying on a table, similar to a massage table, and having two people move her arms and legs in certain patterns for hours. I remember putting a chalklike substance on my hands to keep them from slipping.

Diane, swearing she saw improvement in Angela's behavior, continued the patterning session for four years. I saw none. At the age of twenty-two, Angela, still nonverbal and boasting the same behaviors, was put into a nursing home. Her mom, alone, exhausted and broke, was no longer able to care for her.

As I pulled in the driveway, I heard the phone ring. I flew in the house, leaving Joey in his car seat.

Sue, her voice unusually somber, recited the date and time of the appointment. Numbed by my recent realization, I didn't hear a word she said and quickly cut her off: "Dr. Shaw thinks he's autistic, doesn't she?"

For a moment I couldn't register a sound. Then I heard a faint, "Yes, she does."

A haze of tears, phone calls, family visitors, and disbelievers filled the next twenty-four hours. Even though I knew all along something wasn't right, the impact of 2.3 years of "He is fine; you're just a new mother" turning into "He's autistic" hit me like a Mack truck. Why didn't the doctors see this before? Why didn't I start the log sooner? Why didn't I push harder?

Early the next morning, I was gulping down my third cup of coffee, still sorting everything out in my head, when the phone rang.

"Hello?"

"Hi, Mrs. Burnett?"

"Yes."

"This is T. Berry Brazelton."

"Is this a joke?"

"Excuse me?"

"I'm sorry, Dr. Brazelton, but it's been a long week, and I'm such a huge fan of yours, but I don't know why you're calling my house."

"I heard about your son, Joey, and I would love to take a look at him and be a part of the diagnosis process."

"I'm amazed I'm even talking to you on the phone . . . but why Joey?"

"Joey is 2.3 years old, correct?"

"Yes."

"It's extremely rare that we ever get to diagnose—or for that matter see—a child displaying autistic-like behavior before the age of three, never mind before the age of two and a half. How long have you suspected Joey had a problem?"

"Six weeks old."

Your Exercises

Today we are more plugged in and tuned out than ever before. Headphones, iPhones, texting, tweeting, and an array of other communication and listening tools take us somewhere besides where we are. Preoccupation has become a new form of exercise. I'm a proponent and user of the new technologies, as they offer many benefits. But when I am with my child, I focus on my child. The growth and transformation that children go through from birth to age three happens at the speed of light, and interruptions only take those moments away. There is no rewind. Being attentive to your child requires leaving all your other thoughts, stressors, and concerns so that you can truly focus on your child.

Did you ever have something really important to tell someone—something that meant a lot to you? When you communicated your news, did the recipient focus on what you were saying or was she focused on eating her lunch, answering her cell phone, or looking out the window beyond you, watching something outside? When something like that happens, we question the other person. Even if she says she heard every word, she wasn't really paying attention. Being in the same room isn't enough. You have to focus and concentrate only on your child. In fact, I recommend three to five healthy servings of each other every day.

The Following story illustrates the importance of observation.

From eight months on, Joey was obsessed with street signs—signs that read "Stop," "No Parking," "Slow"; signs that were round, rectangular, octagonal—you name it. I noticed this craze when I walked Joey in the carriage. Every time I walked by a stop sign, or any sign, Joey screeched as if in terrible pain. Nothing consoled him. Dreading our daily walks, I became determined to find out if in fact the street signs caused Joey turmoil.

The next day I took him out in the carriage on our usual route. Soon we came to a stop sign, and the screeching began. This time I stopped the carriage, took Joey out, and lifted him closer to the sign to see if the screeching became louder. Instead he stopped screeching all together and touched his hand to the sign. He rubbed the front and then rubbed the back, all the while displaying the most peaceful look on his face, as if doing this brought him comfort and relief. I put him back in the carriage, and he remained content until we reached the next street sign. And so it went. Every day on our walks I lifted him up (sometimes quite high), and he rubbed the front of each sign and then the back. It seemed to calm him until we got to the next sign.

A half-hour walk turned into a two-hour workout for me. Passersby looked on in puzzlement at our ritual, but I didn't care. It brought Joey (and me) comfort. I purchased miniature street signs, and Joey played with them for hours and hours—lining them up and rubbing them. Soon we took the signs with us in the car, and for the first time since bringing Joey home, Danny and I were able to take Joey with us while we enjoyed a cup of coffee or a glass of wine and an appetizer, as the signs kept Joey content and oblivious to his surroundings for about an hour. I felt victorious. My attentiveness had brought consolation to Joey and small outings—which seemed like weekend getaways—to my husband and me.

Dr. Brazelton and I, in our first conversation, talked on the phone for an hour about the signs and clues that had alerted me along the way. Being attentive to Joey—listening and watching him carefully, with concentration—had brought me to this point.

Even with awareness and documentation, it took 2.3 years for someone to truly take notice of Joey's symptoms. This lack of early diagnosis still persists for families today, but it is not mainly due to mothers' concerns falling on deaf ears. Instead, as parents it's easier for us to talk ourselves out of what we see and witness. The minute we put it in writing or say it out loud, it becomes real to us and to others.

This person—this child—is your world, your utmost reason for living, your purpose. To think some of your child's behaviors will alter how others may view him or her is a lot to bear, I know. But the alternative is much worse. The Autism Society estimates that the cost of lifelong care can be reduced by two-thirds with early diagnosis and intervention—two-thirds![4] Every day we hear how early detection of most diseases increases a positive prognosis by an outrageous percentage. You, as the parent, truly hold the key to your child's successful outcome. The sooner you document your observations and share them with others, the sooner you will get your child the help and services he or she needs. Don't wait another minute. Paying attention and documenting your observations in writing are the first steps to confronting your feelings and defying autism.

The prescreening checklist and observation log on pages 23–26 will alert you to the red flags of autism and assist you in documenting your child's development, including communication, sensory processing, vision, hearing, and gross and fine motor skills. This documentation will help your pediatrician understand and dissect your concerns and foster a better outcome, regardless of your child's diagnosis.

Dr. Brazelton's Recommendation Relative to Early Diagnosis

All research to this point indicates the necessity of diagnosing as early as possible and beginning intensive, evidence-based intervention. Intensive early intervention is the best weapon we have against autism and its related disorders. The brain has breathtaking plasticity—the ability to adapt and change during a child's first few years of life. This is the reason families should not give up hope.

T. Berry Brazelton, MD
Professor of Pediatrics Emeritus, Harvard Medical School
Founder, Brazelton Touchpoints Center

The National Institute of Child Health and Human Development says that further evaluation of your child is warranted if he or she exhibits any of the following:

- Does not babble or coo by twelve months
- Does not gesture (point, wave, grasp) by twelve months
- Does not say single words by sixteen months
- Does not say two-word phrases on his or her own by twenty-four months
- Has any loss of any language or social skill at any age[5]

Initially, in Joey's case, I found his subtle behaviors difficult to fit into the criteria above. For example, Joey would put his bottle on the floor or the table if he wanted more. He never handed the bottle directly to anyone. He didn't babble, but he screeched a funny sound, which I interpreted as his own form of babbling.

Then there are the standard red flags of autism, as noted by the Autism Society:

- Lack of, or delay in, spoken language
- Repetitive use of language or motor mannerisms (for example, hand flapping, twirling objects)
- Little or no eye contact
- Lack of interest in peer relationships
- Lack of spontaneous or make-believe play
- Persistent fixation on parts of objects[6]

To better understand and become more aware of the behaviors listed above, I have created a prescreening checklist and applied the behaviors to daily tasks such as play and sleeping habits. The checklist will help you become more aware of your child's subtle behaviors.

Tips

- *Start the prescreening checklist.* The prescreening checklist is lengthy but thorough. The checklist is designed to serve as a foundation to help you and others better understand your child's needs and behaviors.
- *Maintain the observation log.* The observation log is a supplement to the prescreening checklist. The log is for recording behaviors that are not on the checklist and for documenting concerns about behaviors and needs that are on the checklist. Recording dates and times is very important because the first years of your child's life are filled with change and growth. Keep the observation log by your bed and write the day's observations before you sleep, while they are still fresh in your mind.
- *Trust your gut.* No one knows your child better than you do. You are the expert. The prescreening checklist and the observation log will arm you with the information you need, in a coherent format, to use when you seek medical and educational advice.

Exercises

Go to the sections of the prescreening checklist that most concern you and complete those sections first. The checklist is designed to be completed over time, not all in one day.

Prescreening Checklist[7]
Check the ones that apply to your child.

Touch
- ❏ Becomes fearful, anxious, or aggressive with light or unexpected touch
- ❏ Does not like to be held or cuddled; may arch back, cry, or pull away
- ❏ Distressed when diaper is being or needs to be changed
- ❏ Appears fearful of or avoids standing close to other people (especially in lines)
- ❏ Resists friendly or affectionate touch from anyone besides parents or siblings (and sometimes from them)

❏ A raindrop, water from the shower, or wind blowing on the skin produces adverse and avoidance reactions
❏ Overreacts to minor cuts, scrapes, or bug bites
❏ Avoids touching materials with certain textures (blankets, rugs, stuffed animals)
❏ Refuses to wear new or stiff clothes, clothes with rough textures, turtlenecks, jeans, hats, belts, and other constrictive clothing
❏ Avoids, dislikes, or shows aversion to "messy play" with materials such as sand, mud, water, glue, glitter, Play-Doh, or Funny Foam
❏ Distressed by dirty hands; wants to wipe or wash them frequently
❏ Distressed by seams in socks; may refuse to wear socks
❏ Distressed by clothes rubbing on skin
❏ Distressed about having face washed
❏ Distressed about having hair, toenails, or fingernails cut
❏ Resists brushing teeth; extremely fearful of the dentist
❏ Refuses to walk barefoot on grass or sand
❏ Repeatedly touches surfaces or objects that are soothing (such as a blanket)
❏ Seeks out surfaces and textures that provide strong tactile feedback, such as rubbing head on a carpet

Hearing
❏ Appears to be deaf
❏ Seems to hear sometimes but not other times
❏ Distracted by sounds not normally noticed by others (fans, heaters, ticking of clocks, humming of lights or refrigerators)
❏ Fearful of the sound of vacuum cleaners, hair dryers, squeaky shoes, barking dogs, or flushing toilets (especially in public bathrooms)
❏ Startled or distracted by loud or unexpected sounds
❏ Bothered or distracted by background environmental sounds (lawn mowing or outside construction)
❏ Runs away, cries, or covers ears in reaction to loud or unexpected sounds
❏ Often does not respond to verbal cues or to his or her name being called
❏ Appears oblivious to certain sounds
❏ Appears confused about where a sound is coming from

Sight
- ❑ Sensitive to bright lights; squints, covers eyes, cries, or gets headaches in response to bright light
- ❑ Has difficulty keeping eyes focused on the task or activity at hand for an appropriate amount of time
- ❑ Easily distracted by visual stimuli such as movement, decorations, toys, windows, and doorways
- ❑ Avoids eye contact
- ❑ Difficulty controlling eye movement to track and follow moving objects

Speech
- ❑ Little or no vocalizing or babbling as an infant
- ❑ Constantly repeats words that you or someone else says (echolalia)
- ❑ The loss of words previously spoken
- ❑ Delayed speech
- ❑ Cannot explain what he or she wants
- ❑ Doesn't follow directions

Movement
- ❑ Odd movement patterns
- ❑ Overly active, uncooperative, or resistant

Play
- ❑ Doesn't know how to play with toys
- ❑ Does the same actions over and over with toys; can't move on to other means of play
- ❑ Prefers to play alone
- ❑ Gets toys for him- or herself only
- ❑ Participates in repetitive play for hours (lining up toy cars or blocks or watching one movie over and over)
- ❑ Not interested in other children

Taste
- ❑ Is a picky eater, only eating certain tastes and textures; avoids mixed textures or hot or cold foods; resists new foods
- ❑ Refuses to eat certain foods because of their smell

Sleep
- ❑ Excessive irritability, fussiness, or colic as an infant
- ❑ Can't be calmed or soothed by a pacifier, comfort object, or caregiver
- ❑ Can't go from sleeping to being awake without distress
- ❑ Requires excessive help from a caregiver (rubbing back or head, rocking, long walks, or car rides) to fall asleep

Observation Log

Use the space below to note any behavior that concerns you, no matter how insignificant it may seem. If it is concerning, it is not insignificant. Trust your observations.

Date: _____ Time: _____

Observed: _____

_____

Date: _____ Time: _____

Observed: _____

_____

Date: _____ Time: _____

Observed: _____

_____

Date: _____ Time: _____

Observed: _____

_____

Step Three:
ACCEPT

/Accept/ **To acknowledge a fact or truth
and come to terms with it**

Joey's appointment at Boston Children's Hospital came a day after the first snow of December. Sue, Joey's pediatric nurse, had made the appointment with Roger Carter, and beyond his name, we knew nothing more except for the date and time.

The week prior to our visit, images of my past outings to Children's augmented my fears, making me sleepless. At five years old, I visited my eldest brother, Joe, there. Lying face-up, strapped to a striker bed no wider than his own body, Joe had screws burrowed into his head and feet, affixing him to the bed's metal contraptions like a fixture on a crucifix.

Joe lay there for two weeks while the bed rotated every two hours, alternating his view between the ceiling and the floor. The purpose was, my mom told me on our ride home, to stretch his spine prior to surgery to correct his severe scoliosis (curvature of the spine). After surgery Joe exchanged his crucifix for a full-length body cast, which he remained in for six months.

At thirteen I visited my neighbor's fifteen-year-old daughter Mary, afflicted with anorexia. At eighty-five pounds and near death, with her mother asleep in the chair by her bed, Mary looked ancient and beaten.

The tubes running in and out of her displayed more girth than the remaining mass of her body.

At twenty I visited my five-year-old niece Sarah, who'd been diagnosed with an inoperable brain tumor, sleeping soundly in the intensive care ward after her fifteen-hour shunt surgery. Her mom, my sister Kathy, was at the foot of the bed, secretly trying to strike a deal with God.

At thirty-five I thought about Joey needing to be diagnosed at Boston Children's Hospital. I knew his issues were serious, and I felt frightened.

Arriving thirty minutes early, as Dr. Shaw had suggested, Danny and I parked in the garage across the street and trod through the snowy surplus from the previous day's storm. The circular drive in and out of Boston Children's main entrance looked more like access to an airport terminal than to a hospital. We passed by patient drop-off and pickup signs, piled up suitcases, and a double row of parked yellow city cabs. The drivers exchanged a dialogue only they understood. Ground-to-ceiling glass revolving doors summoned us to enter, packing their participants in like cattle. For a fleeting moment, images of *Schindler's List* Nazi camps flashed in my head, we being the chosen.

As we busted into the foyer, all eyes were on us, the newest herd. The existing livestock, exhibiting cream-of-wheat complexions with raccoon-rimmed eyes, appeared broken in and branded; the endless cups of caffeine and plasticlike pastries offered no freedom from their newly fenced-in lives. I held Joey's hand tightly, whispering under my breath with each step, "We're only visiting," as the three of us made our way to the open staircase at the far side of the foyer. Walking by a wall of windows, I watched as life continued on the other side.

At the top of the staircase, we found several hallways, each one appearing longer and grayer than the next. A constant parade of white coats in all shapes and sizes marched by with purpose and determination while trying to keep rhythm with the constant ringing of telephones and loudspeaker announcements. Danny stopped a harried nurse to get directions. She told us that Dr. Carter's office was on the fifth floor in the psychiatric and psychology unit. We boarded the elevator and found our way to Dr. Carter's receptionist. She looked all of fifteen years old, her coal black hair pausing at her shoulders and then continuing down, falling in her lap. She had huge black eyes, olive skin, and a Middle Eastern accent. I gave her Joey's name and information as Danny helped Joey line up his signs in the waiting area.

I had a million questions and I had none. The longer we waited, the more I questioned the notes I'd taken about Joey's behavior. Doubt set in. What am I doing? My child is not mentally ill or crazy. Have I sentenced him to a life of being poked and prodded by my mothering mistakes? I felt a powerful urge to whisk Joey in my arms and run for the elevators, proclaiming I'd made a terrible error. I started to rise. Just then a young man looking no more than twenty years old came toward us, introducing himself as Roger Carter. Barely my height of 5 feet 7 inches, with tanned skin and straight black hair, he struggled to put his hand out while balancing his Diet Coke and clipboard. Assuming it was laundry day for whites in his dorm, as he wore only jeans and a button-down shirt, I shook his hand, his sparkling college ring cutting into my fingers.

As I started to panic at the thought of a child diagnosing my child, a woman in her thirties, wearing a white coat and stethoscope, stepped around the corner. She had an earthy glow, with long brown hair and no makeup. She wore a long tapestry skirt and boots, giving her an easy, casual appearance that simultaneously commanded respect and reverence. She put her hand out to Danny, introducing herself as Dr. Karen Levine, head of child psychology at Boston Children's Hospital. Our apparent blatant relief embarrassed Dr. Carter. His face instantly flushed. After introductions, the doctors led us to a room filled with toys and books. It had a large round table in the center and offered six small chairs, all child size. We sucked in our stomachs as we squished into our seats in unison.

Oblivious to the treasures in the room, Joey held tightly to my shirt with one hand while lining up his signs with the other. Dr. Levine's voice, calming yet resilient, rose and fell like a Joni Mitchell song. She talked to us while shuffling black-and-white puzzles and picture boards Joey's way. Joey seemed to respond to her indirectly by performing the small tasks she strategically placed before him. Dr. Carter interjected here and there while taking notes, as directed by Dr. Levine, who continued this ritual until Joey's hand flapping and nervous gestures signaled that he had had enough.

I was surprised that the tasks had held Joey's attention for a full twenty minutes. Dr. Levine revealed that the stimuli gave Joey the same relief and feeling of control as his signs did, thus his lengthy attention. The doctors asked us to wait in the room and then left. Danny walked Joey up and down the hallways to ease some of his nervousness while I waited for the doctors. Finally the doctors returned, transporting papers and pamphlets in hand. Dr. Levine spoke first.

"I would like Joey to see Ann Stroble, one of the chief speech and language pathologists here at Children's, for a more in-depth needs diagnosis." The needs diagnosis, she went on to explain, "is a two-step process. First, through additional testing and your input, we can more thoroughly understand behaviors particular to Joey and the daily challenges you both face. We then take those findings and determine the best way to meet those needs." Danny, now standing in the doorway, Joey squirming in his arms, blurted out, "What is actually wrong with our son? What does Joey have?"

Dr. Carter answered, "Joey has pervasive developmental disorder (PDD), which is in the autism family, or spectrum. Autism is a developmental brain disorder characterized by impaired social interaction and communication skills. Pervasive developmental disorder refers to a group of conditions that involve delays in the development of many basic skills, most notably the ability to socialize with others, to communicate, and to use imagination. Children with these conditions often are confused in their thinking and generally have problems understanding the world around them. Limited range of activities and interests is the most characteristic and best studied PDD. Children with PDD vary widely in abilities, intelligence, and behaviors. Some children do not speak at all, others speak in limited phrases or conversations, and some have relatively normal language development. Repetitive play skills and limited social skills are generally evident as well. Unusual responses to sensory information— loud noises, lights. . . ."

Seeing the confusion on our faces, Dr. Levine gracefully interrupted Dr. Carter. "I think Joey will be high functioning. You, as a parent, have already played a key role by providing your pediatrician with documented information about Joey's behavior at home. Based on his early age at diagnosis, he has a good chance. Continue to be aware and attentive and start to ascertain Joey's needs as you see them from your perspective. That information will be valuable for the needs diagnosis."

Just then Joey reached his limit and began to squeal and screech. Danny, needing to get out of there as much as Joey did, volunteered to take him outside to the car.

Dr. Levine continued: "I would like to take him as a patient and follow his progress. I know it's a distance for you to come, but I think it will be worth it. I would also like to come to your house to witness Joey in his own environment. I can make the appointment for you with Dr. Stroble, and we can work out a schedule of how often to meet, maybe once per month or six weeks for you to bring Joey here, whatever time will allow. How does that sound, Mrs. Burnett?"

Fixated on her words, "I think Joey will be high functioning," I replied, "I'll do whatever it takes."

"Good, because it will take that continued solid attitude and energy for you and your husband to get through this and to provide Joey with a positive outcome." She got up and left to get the schedule and an appointment card for Dr. Stroble.

I sat there thinking about my past excursions to Children's, the strength of the people involved, and their successful outcomes. My brother Joe, now forty-eight, healthy, straight, and tall; my neighbor's daughter Mary, now married with two children of her own; and my niece Sarah, now twenty years old, a college graduate and a survivor of many more shunt surgeries.

I thought about a paper I had written in eighth-grade English class entitled "Get a Grip." It was about emotional strength and the importance of having it. I knew now why I had picked that topic. Could I live up to my grade-A paper? Did I have what I said it would take? I couldn't even remember what I had written. The longer Dr. Levine's return took, the more anxious I grew, the noise from my knee rapping into the tiny table now at an annoying decibel. I imagined Danny growing irritable as he drove around the city, trying to console Joey. I felt exhausted and overwhelmed.

"Are you going to be okay?" Dr. Carter interrupted my thoughts. I wiped my face and tried to pull myself together. He got up, walked over, and sat down next to me. "It's not your fault, you know."

"I'm sorry?"

"I could see it in your eyes during the visit. You blame yourself. There's nothing you could have done to prevent it, and you didn't cause it. I can guarantee you that."

Right before my eyes, this twenty-year-old kid doctor offered the hug and shoulder I had needed to cry on for the past four months. Somehow the location of his white coat no longer mattered.

Four days later: An older, lean man of average height, boasting a full head of gray hair, walked purposely toward us, followed by a small entourage of seven white-coated younger men and women, all carrying clipboards and pens.

"Dr. Brazelton," the man stated as he put his hand out to shake mine. His face exuded compassion, and his eyes and smile comforted me. I knew immediately why mothers poured their hearts out to him. He looked like he genuinely cared.

"Anne Burnett, and this is my husband, Danny, and our son, Joey."

He took my hand in his and cupped it. "So glad we connected. It is not often we get to see a child so young." Right then I wanted to say, "Oh please, please help me. My son has been diagnosed with PDD, and I might have done something wrong as a mom, and my family doesn't understand, and I don't know where my husband is at with all of this." Instead I just smiled back. He shook Danny's hand and gently touched Joey's sneaker high up in Danny's arms.

"Let's go in." He opened a door off the hallway. It led into a small oval room with a square toddler table and four chairs in the center, nothing else. "This handsome group behind—these practitioners and student practitioners—will observe Joey, with me, from the observation deck." Dr. Brazelton motioned to our right. A large tinted window covered the middle of the upper half of the wall on the right side of the room, and I wondered if someone was watching us then. "Leslie Dockham will conduct the evaluation here in this room with Joey, with you and Danny attending." A young woman with ivory skin and strawberry blond hair to her shoulders stepped out of the group and introduced herself as Leslie. Expressionless, she pulled out tan-framed glasses from the pocket of her white lab coat and placed them on her face. She walked across the room, pulled out a drawer from within the wall, and took out puzzles, pictures, and cubes, all shapes and sizes.

"We will converse after the evaluation," Dr. Brazelton whispered, as if the evaluation were already underway. He excused himself from the room, his entourage in tow. I could hear them filing into the room above us, making me feel self-conscious, while Joey and Danny appeared to be oblivious.

Leslie immediately began performing small tasks with Joey—sorting cubes, pulling puzzles apart and putting them back together, completing black-and-white pictures. Danny and I looked blankly at each other, trying to interpret the significance of each function. Twenty minutes later, Joey reached his limit, ending the evaluation. Leslie picked up the materials quickly and placed them back in the drawer. She removed her glasses in silence and directed us back into the hallway. At the same time, Dr. Brazelton came out an adjacent door and walked toward us.

"Joey is an adorable little boy," he began. "It's great that you brought him in this young; a lot can be done at this early age. You should think about sending him to the May Institute.

My heart sank—*the May Institute?* Although I later found out what amazing work the May Institute accomplishes for autistic children, at that time I knew only about its year-round residential care unit on Cape Cod for children and adolescents who had suffered brain trauma and another residential program on the North Shore for autistic children.

"Dr. Brazelton, I'm a black-and-white kind of guy," Danny nervously blurted out. "Is Joey ever going to talk?"

"They're doing great things at the May, making great strides."

Danny, unsatisfied with Dr. Brazelton's response, asked the question again. "Yes . . . but will he talk?"

"Anything is possible," Dr. Brazelton smiled benignly. Danny, I imagined feeling too frustrated to continue, appeared to tune out of the conversation. He'd politely nod from time to time, but, as far as I could tell, he was no longer present.

"I want the best for Joey, the best services and care, but I can't picture him at the May. He . . . well, I believe Joey is going to talk and is brighter than we know. He has these street signs," I went on, pulling Joey's signs from my purse. Joey immediately reached for them. "When he's playing with them, he's so intense, so focused. I just feel the May Institute may be too segregated for him. I think he would benefit from being around normal functioning children too."

Danny did a double take as he spun around to look at me, this woman spewing off words as if she knew what she were doing and talking about, relief washing over his face. I surprised myself and yet felt confident in my perceptions. Then a twinge of doubt crept in. "I'm sorry, Dr. Brazelton, I don't know what I am talking about. You're the doctor; it's just a feeling I have about Joey."

"Never apologize for knowing your child. You're the authority about your son. Embrace and use that to Joey's benefit. Your knowledge of your son got you here in the first place. Use your strength and confidence in yourself to continue to guide him. I've witnessed your son for twenty minutes; you've witnessed him for more than two years. Believe in what you see and feel. I do believe, however, from my expertise and years of experience, that the sooner you can get Joey intense services—communication, language, behavior, and sensory therapies—the more pronounced his progress will be. Given this information, find a program you can picture Joey in, one that's integrated, with a fair ratio of normal functioning and challenged children. If Joey is comfortable in his environment, he'll flourish."

"How will I know he's comfortable?"

"He'll show you."

Danny, wearing a look of both pride and acquittal, grabbed my hand in the car and held onto it all the way home. I realized that I truly did have the power and strength to take Joey where he needed to be to fulfill his potential. I leaned back and looked up through the sunroof at the clear blue December sky—my limit looking back at me.

Your Exercises

Over the years I've read numerous books about autism, both clinical and personal stories. Inevitably, the authors use descriptive words such as grief, denial, anger, devastation, and anguish, which always strikes me as odd. These words don't describe the children diagnosed with autism but rather their parents, families, and caregivers.

Parents need to grieve when something tragic happens to their child. Grieving is a normal and necessary process for healing. Successfully mourning your child's diagnosis gives you a new sense of self-confidence. You come to believe you can work through any difficulties that get in your way. The deep anguish your child's diagnosis presents leads you to understand how connected you are to your child and how that wonderful bond will give you the strength to move forward and be positive.

Many parents, however, permanently grieve their child's diagnosis, as if they have succumbed to it as a life sentence. Recently, Lisa Jo Rudy, author of the column "Autism Spectrum Disorders" for www.about.com, ran a poll and noted that her readers were most interested in success stories from parents. Yet her stats indicated that the actual success stories available on her site were the least read, so she asked why. The responses she received shocked her—yet I continue to meet parents who react this way:

> Autism is supposed to be life-long, so success can mean many different things depending on who's telling the story.
> — S.

> Autism is a life sentence and so very difficult for others to comprehend.
> — L.

> I suppose this is going to sound terrible, but at this point (my daughter was just diagnosed) success stories don't comfort me at all.
> — K.

When you learn that autism is part of your family, life does not end; it changes. It is up to you, as a parent, to remember that. Remember that as soon as you accept your challenge as an opportunity to realize your capabilities as a parent and as a person, you empower yourself and others. Then you can move your child forward and provide him with a rich and rewarding outcome.

Empowering Advice from Dr. Brazelton

Parents of children who have just been diagnosed with autism might have a difficult time adjusting to the diagnosis. So many questions and thoughts run through your head that it can be difficult to focus. The diagnosis of autism for your child is not a conviction. Rather it provides an opportunity for you to grow and learn as a parent and to watch your child flourish. Trust your instincts and focus less on what's wrong and more on what's right.

T. Berry Brazelton, MD
Professor of Pediatrics Emeritus, Harvard Medical School
Founder, Brazelton Touchpoints Center

Acceptance has two layers. In addition to accepting the diagnosis, you need to take ownership of what is before you. Initially, I didn't know where to put the ownership, so I blamed myself. I knew at six weeks that Joey's behavior warranted concern, yet when I heard the diagnosis, I was bewildered. Human nature is funny. We kid ourselves into thinking we have come to terms with something when we are just going through the motions. Not until I met Dr. Brazelton and faced the first decision about Joey's future did I fully understand and accept what taking ownership of Joey's diagnosis meant to me, my family, my friends, and Joey. Taking ownership meant taking responsibility for providing Joey with the best possible outcome, regardless of what that entailed. Taking responsibility meant fully and quickly accepting this change in our lives, so as not to delay Joey's opportunity for well-being.

Dr. Brazelton showed me the importance of acceptance by relying on me as the decision maker for my child. Now you have to be the decision maker for yours. Complete the acceptance exercise and learn to put aside your fears. Accept and embrace your child's diagnosis, as it is an opportunity for you to go beyond your perceived limits and become the person—the mother or the father—you are truly meant to be.

Tips

- *Finish what you start.* Before starting the exercise, make sure you will be able to complete it without interruption.
- *Take your time.* Choose a time when you will not have to rush through the exercise.
- *Get relaxed and in a good place first.* Take a walk or do some yoga.
- *Be open and honest.* You are the only person who needs to see your responses.

Exercises

Complete the following exercises to gain a better understanding of how you can accept your child's diagnosis so you can move toward a positive outcome.

1. List three positive feelings you have about your child today.

    a. _____

    b. _____

    c. _____

2. What feelings do you have when facing your child's diagnosis? List ten—for example, "blame," "disappointment," "strength," "motivation," "anger," "fear," "optimism."

    a. _____

    b. _____

    c. _____

    d. _____

    e. _____

    f. _____

    g. _____

    h. _____

    i. _____

    j. _____

3. If your child has been diagnosed with autism, what four areas of your life will require the most change, and how will they be altered? Example, "My work schedule will change because I will have to work fewer hours so I can take my son to speech therapy three times per week."

    a. _____

    b. _____

    c. _____

    d. _____

4. How will the four changes above benefit your child's outcome?

    a. _____

    b. _____

    c. _____

    d. _____

5. Based on your answers to Question 4, where do you imagine your child's progress will be in six months?

    a. _____

    b. _____

    c. _____

    d. _____

6. Based on your answers in Question 5, list six positive feelings
    you have knowing you can be a major contributor to your child's
    progress.

    a. _____

    b. _____

    c. _____

    d. _____

    e. _____

    f. _____

7. Go back to Question 2 and cross out the feelings you no longer feel
    about your child's diagnosis.

8. List six positive feelings you are having about your child today.

    a. _____

    b. _____

    c. _____

    d. _____

    e. _____

    f. _____

Step Four:
ASCERTAIN

/*Ascertain*/ **To find out something with certainty**

Ann Stroble stood 5 feet 11 inches, with stone-cut features and thick, healthy gray hair styled to her shoulders. She wore a navy blue suit, navy blue heels, and a white silk blouse, looking more like an executive from Fidelity than a chief speech and language pathologist. Dignified in mannerisms and stance, she began testing Joey's speech and language skills while I listened and observed. Joey, not having any speech, required visuals comprised of small foam boards with pictures of a cup, a dog, a ball, a cat, and so on. To see if he could understand her, Dr. Stroble asked Joey to point to a certain picture. Then she asked questions such as, "Which one of these pictures would you pour juice into?" She tried to keep her questions as short as possible. At times I thought Joey understood, but other times he would be terribly wrong, leaving no clear pattern of understanding, as Dr. Stroble termed it.

Since this was my third visit to Boston Children's Hospital within two months, I had thoroughly prepared myself for the appointment. I had two months to read and absorb every medical journal I could find on PDD. I asked for copies of the notes from Joey's visit to Dr. Levine and notes from Dr. Shaw, which, as a parent, I was entitled to. I gathered my prescreening checklist and observation log (see Chapter 2) and began combining all the information into an inventory of behaviors. I made notes about what I felt Joey would require in a preschool program when he turned three and any early intervention services he would be entitled to until then.

With this information in hand, Dr. Stroble and I worked together to decide what services would best benefit Joey's behaviors, since people with autism are not all the same. They respond to various treatments based on their communication, behavior, and developmental levels.

Collaboratively, Dr. Stroble and I came up with the following recommendations for Joey:

1. A small, integrated, language-based classroom should be provided, with teachers who have had special training and experience working with autistic and PDD children. It is important that he be able to obtain individual help throughout the day, as needed. In addition, it is extremely important that there be a small teacher-to-child ratio. It is also extremely important that this be continued through the summer and that the parents be involved.

2. Speech and language therapy is recommended several times weekly in short sessions (20–30 minutes) within the program. Mrs. Burnett should be actively involved in the therapy program in order to ensure continuity/carryover at home. Mrs. Burnett should work with the speech pathologist to find everyday routines and activities that can be modified to facilitate Joey's communication development. Modifications include slower pacing, active involvement, visual cues, and language simplification.

3. Interactive alphabet and book activities should be used with Joey. Home read-aloud sessions should be kept brief, stimulating, and attuned to Joey's interest level and attention span in the beginning. This should always be fun-filled and pleasurable.

4. Desensitization needs to be implemented both at home and in the classroom to aid and diminish Joey's fears of fire, transitions, and car braking as well as his tactile rigidness. Such activities as lighting one candle every night at dinner and driving in the driveway lightly touching on the brakes can begin at home.

5. Representational and pretend play skills should be fostered in an effort to encourage development of Joey's imagination. These activities should be enjoyable for all participants. A favored stuffed animal can be

included in everyday activities, such as eating, dressing, and so on. Joey's favorite toys can be brought to the classroom at special times. Adults can respond to Joey's play and actions and model slightly more elaborate forms of play with him. These are excellent tools to help him develop auditory attention and direction following. These activities have the additional advantage of providing enjoyable adult–child interaction.

6.   The present findings need to be viewed within the context of the findings of other specialists who have seen Joey. The use of computer-based learning programs should also be explored.

7.   Joey should be seen for speech and language consultations on a regular basis.

8.   Early intervention services should be implemented for Joey, to include applied behavioral analysis (ABA) now until the age of three.

This group of recommendations became the springboard for securing the best services (suited for Joey) available.

In addition to obtaining a thorough needs assessment for Joey, we talked about the need to continually reassess Joey. What at first seems unreasonable and not suitable for Joey may eventually make the best sense. Raising your autistic child will present plenty of opportunities to reassess available resources and to search for new ones. It is important to be open-minded and flexible during this process. Each time you find a solution to a problem or situation your child is confronted with, your child is benefiting. In our case, the benefit was following up on Dr. Stroble's recommendation for early intervention services.

Early Intervention

Joey clung to the last living square of his baby blanket as I lightly waltzed him across the living room floor to Natalie Cole's rendition of "Unforgettable." Chomping on the worn, oversize pacifier that hung halfway out of his mouth, like a detective smoking a cigar, Joey earnestly tried to keep watch for the intrusion of sleep, his eyelids falling prey each time the song repeated. The record number of plays being eleven, I braced my arms to hold out for at least one more round.

The nightly routine—a soothing bubble bath courtesy of Johnson's lavender baby soap, getting into cozy Grover pajamas, three readings of *Happy and Sad, Grouchy and Glad,* and a warmed bottle of Alimentum, all followed by Nat King Cole songs sung by his daughter Natalie—sedated me too, and I felt my body giving in to the weight of the day. Ultimately, sleep came for us both.

March's first winds rattled me awake, my clock reading 5:50 a.m. Joey's internal alarm normally woke him every day at 5:30. I headed to his room, excited at this potential improvement in his routine and peeked in . . . no Joey. Hearing Danny showering in the bathroom down the hall, I assumed Joey had made his way there. No. I ran down the hallway, frantically stumbling over toys uncollected from the day before, my heart now racing, my hand clutching my chest. Down the stairs, past the living room windows, my eyes caught a glimpse of white movement through the faint morning light outside. There in the backyard, dressed in just his diaper, swinging on the swing . . . Joey. His body, flushed from the 38-degree weather, moving back and forth with the wind. I flew out the door, swept him up, flung my bathrobe around his frozen back, and ran inside.

Danny made his way downstairs, towel-draped and dripping, appearing to me to be too frustrated to speak. That night after work, he installed locks at the tops of the doors, stopping Joey from getting out of the house on his own.

Joey's high energy level seemed to adversely affect everything: his ability to focus, his attention span, and—most importantly—his safety. His inability to regulate his energy also caused him to tantrum—a lot. His screaming, screeching, head-banging fits exhausted me more than him. On many occasions, half-full carts sat abandoned in Stop and Shop's aisles, a product of Joey's tantrums. One morning at home he threw tantrums twenty-two separate times before 9:00 a.m. It was four months before Joey would turn three and be eligible to start a preschool program. I knew we needed more than the Band-Aid of security locks at the tops of doors. We needed Joey to change his behavior.

Ann Stroble had recommended early intervention for Joey during the needs assessment, yet I had dismissed it. I felt it would serve no purpose if we obtained it for only a few months, until he turned three, and quite honestly I felt nervous at the prospect of a stranger coming in the house, into our lives and into Joey's world. I worried it would be traumatic for all of us.

The principle of early intervention is to provide appropriate therapies for children with disabilities, to minimize their delays, and to maximize their chances of reaching normal milestones in development. Early intervention can begin at birth or first diagnosis and continues until age three.

At Joey's initial diagnosis, Dr. Levine had suggested that we consider ABA therapy for Joey's high energy level, but my family—mainly my sister Mary—had "feared" me out of trying it. Mary, a special needs aid in Minnesota, described ABA as applied shock treatment, and all I could envision was something out of *One Flew over the Cuckoo's Nest*. But worn down by Joey's behavior and fearing for his safety, I decided to research ABA on my own.

I went back through my notes from our visit with Ann Stroble and found the names of three agencies that provided ABA therapy. The first two I contacted had lengthy waiting lists. The third agency, Beacon Services in Milford, could send someone out to review our case and start therapy within a week. I registered Joey and spent the week pacing and cleaning.

On Monday a light blue Toyota Corolla pulled into our driveway. A young woman in her mid-twenties got out, went to the rear of the car, and opened the trunk. Ten minutes went by, and still she hovered behind the trunk door. I felt sick. My sister Mary was right. I thought the woman must be out there pulling together wires and tools to zap Joey and gathering ropes to tie me up while she did it. The ring of the doorbell pulled me out of my *Mission Impossible* episode and back to reality. I opened the door to find a freckled, wholesome face looking up at me. A mere speck of a girl stood there carrying what appeared to be a stuffed, blue-checkered pillowcase in her right hand, a folded poster board under her left arm, and a little red treasure chest in her left hand. I welcomed her in, and she gestured hello while struggling to release a hand to shake mine.

"Anne Burnett. Nice to meet you," I said, closing the door before Joey could escape between us.

"Lisa Wharton. Great to meet you, too."

This young woman with the voice of a mouse is never going to be able to command Joey to focus for even a millisecond, I thought, sighing under my breath, frustrated at the pointless morning I anticipated. "I thought we could meet in the family room."

"That's fine," Lisa replied.

Blanketed in wall-to-wall carpeting, our large family room held an abundance of books and toys methodically tucked away in their assigned areas. I tried to keep only a few toys out at once, since too many seemed to over stimulate Joey. A comfy brown sectional ran along the corner of one side of the room and a toddler table and chairs filled the other.

Lisa began setting up shop on the toddler table. She opened up the trifold poster board and set it on the table. The numbers one through ten ran down the left side of the board. Vertically were ten coin slots, one for each number. She placed the red treasure chest in the middle of the table.

Lisa explained the ABA therapy she had chosen for Joey. "I like to refer to it as 'pennies from heaven,' or at least that's what some of the moms started calling it after I began therapy with their children," Lisa proudly stated.

She placed the pillowcase next to the chair she occupied. I strained to see the contents as she continued with her explanation.

"Basically, it works like this. Joey will sit here at the table with me. I'll have him start by performing three small tasks, such as matching two blocks, placing one puzzle piece, and pointing out one picture. For every three small tasks he completes, he gets to pull one penny off the board and place it in the treasure chest. Once he has two pennies, he can take a break and play with one of the toys that reside in my pillowcase." I calculated: two pennies, six tasks.

"How many pennies do you suppose he'll be able to get up to at some point?"

"I'll have him up to ten pennies by the end of four weeks," Lisa stated with confidence.

"Ten pennies? You mean he'll complete thirty tasks? He'll be sitting in that chair completing thirty tasks before he can get up and play with one toy? How long does he get to play with the toy he chooses?"

"Four minutes."

Lisa came three times per week for an hour to an hour and a half at a time. Week after week, she increased the penny limit and brought an array of toys for Joey to choose from. She gave Joey a thirty-second timeout if he did not comply by returning to his chair at the end of the four-minute playtime. Even with our share of meltdowns, the improvement in Joey's ability to focus proved impressive. By the end of the fourth week, Joey sat for thirty tasks and proudly placed ten pennies in the red treasure chest. I had an entirely new opinion about the benefits of ABA therapy.

Your Exercise

Your newly diagnosed child is the same child she was the day before the diagnosis. The label "autism" is just your key for accessing services and treatment for your child.

Having completed the prescreening checklist and the observation log, you now have concrete information about your child and her behaviors. Once you know your child's specific diagnosis, you can read up on the disorder and gain the confidence and knowledge needed to request additional services. After researching PDD on my own and knowing Joey's behaviors, I knew that a year-round, highly structured program would be the best fit for him. He needed small class sizes and preferably no cafeteria,

A Psychologist's Sound Instruction

Children with autism require a multitude of assessments for the following reasons:

- To get various services through school
- To track their progress
- To follow the recommendations of prior assessments

Some assessments are productive and useful, others are stressful and useful, and some are stressful and useless. As a parent, you should come away from an assessment with something solid—either a practical new strategy, a solution to a challenge you are facing, a piece of information or a new understanding about your child, a new perspective, or a resource. Alternatively, an assessment might teach something useful about your child to people who will be working with him. In the course of a productive assessment, parents and assessors together build a shared understanding of some aspect of the child.

The following strategies can increase the likelihood that the assessment process will be useful for you and your child:

1.   Let the person doing the assessment know if you—or whoever referred you to the assessment—have specific questions. For instance, you might take your child for a speech evaluation and not care so much about the age level of his vocabulary but really want strategies for increasing how much he looks at you when communicating or want to learn what you can do to help him communicate more with peers at school. The speech therapist might have a standard test battery, but knowing your specific concerns, she will be able to think about these issues and use information from the assessment to make recommendations.

2.   Use video clips when possible. Many children don't act like themselves in testing or assessment situations. They feel anxious, overly excited, or distressed and hence function at a more impaired level than is typical. Or they might be on their best behavior, so the assessing person doesn't get a clear picture. Or your concerns might be about situations that won't occur at the assessment, such as how your child functions at the grocery store or at home with his sister. To make sure the person doing the assessment is able to see your child as he is typically, make short video clips using your phone, camera, or laptop. If you don't have a device with a camera, a school or therapy program might be able to loan you one. Film your child at mealtime, playtime, or bedtime. Capture typical situations or times of concern. Be careful to not include other children without parental permission (for example, at school) and do not compromise your child's privacy or dignity in any way. Capturing your child's behavior on video can greatly reduce the stress of going to an assessment. Edit video clips down to short meaningful segments to increase the likelihood that the person doing the assessment will view them. This way you can also show rather than describe your concerns.

Karen Levine, PhD
Instructor, Harvard Medical School,
Cofounder and Codirector, Autism Program,
Boston Children's Hospital;
Cofounder and Codirector, Autism Center,
Cambridge Health Alliance;
Recipient, 2010 Federation for Children with
Special Needs Founders Award

since noise and food smells troubled him immensely. Seemingly insignificant details such as these might be major contributors to the comfort and overall success of your child, so don't be afraid to speak up and share your concerns and recommendations.

It is also important to be open to services, therapies, and treatments, even if you feel apprehensive or fearful about them. Researching them for yourself will give you more confidence and certainty and a broader approach to dealing with your child's disorder.

Tips

- *Do your homework.* Take time to read up on your child's diagnosis prior to obtaining services or securing a needs assessment. Research therapies and services; your commitment of time now will pay off in the future.
- *Be prepared.* For every appointment, bring a fresh list of concerns and observations; be an active participant in the process. Add to the prescreening checklist any new behaviors you've witnessed since your previous visit. Update your observation log often.
- *Be informative.* Establish and build relationships with your child's doctors, counselors, and specialists. Tell them of new services and therapies you have heard of and acquaint them with new approaches that have worked for you at home or in the classroom.
- *Communicate.* The more information you bring to the conversation, the more information professionals will give back. It is important that parents and professionals work together for the child's benefit. While professionals will use their experience and training to make recommendations about your child's treatment options, you have unique knowledge about her needs and abilities. Take this knowledge into account for a more individualized course of action.

Exercise

Consider the following list of questions when you are developing your child's needs assessment. Identify concerns you would like to include in your child's assessment and note them below. Bring the needs inventory (see below), prescreening checklist (page 23), and observation log (page 26) to your child's needs assessment appointment.

Classroom Concerns
In a classroom setting, does your child

- have difficulty in group activities, including play and games;
- react to overstimulation;
- need an escape from stressful situations;
- benefit from clear structure and a set daily routine (including for play);
- need to be addressed individually at all times;
- have difficulty with transitions and need a warning of any impending change of routine or switch of activity?

Needs Inventory

Home: _____

_____

_____

_____

Classroom: _____

_____

_____

_____

Environment (outdoors and in public): _____

_____

_____

_____

_____

Early intervention: _____

_____

_____

_____

_____

Therapies: _____

_____

_____

_____

_____

Step Five:
ADAPT

/Adapt/ **To put oneself in harmony
with changed circumstances**

The town we lived in did not offer an integrated preschool, meaning a mix of normal functioning and developmentally delayed students. Our town had two classrooms, one with "normal" functioning toddlers and a separate "special needs" class, in which all the toddlers possessed a challenge of some sort. Joey needed the combination classroom to learn to assimilate normal peer behaviors or, at a minimum, to be exposed to them.

Attentive to Joey's needs and accepting his diagnosis, I knew immediately that Danny and I needed to adapt. Adapt, in this case, meant moving to a town that offered an integrated preschool. Integrated preschools existed only in public school settings and only for residents in the corresponding towns. By state law, we could request that our town send Joey to preschool in a town offering integration, but time did not allow for this. We could not advocate on Joey's behalf until September, when school reconvened. Concerned that time constraints would slow Joey's progress, I convinced my husband that we needed to move.

Moving confronted us with an intricate task on many levels. First, we had just put the final touches on—and our last penny into—our

250-plus-year-old home on four-and-a-half acres. The house sat across the street from a marsh, a serene and simple habitat that attracted a daily showing of bird-watchers and artists. The marsh was the one and only amenity that had sold me on this property. The antique home, condemned when we purchased it and now resurrected, stood like a monument to my husband's hard labor. It boasted 14-foot ceilings, stained-glass windows, original hardwood throughout, hand-carved moldings, and a banister on the stairs that turned and curved, making our entranceway the perfect prom promenade. My husband has a true gift for restoration, and I now realize how that must have played into his frustration about moving. Aside from leaving a home he loved and had practically rebuilt, we moved for reasons Danny could not simply refurbish or repair.

Second, we had family in this town, as well as two babysitters who understood Joey and gave us some respite—my mother and a dear friend's daughter, Maria Spinale.

Leaving our beloved home tested our commitment as parents and as a couple. We had rebuilt the house together as a team, a unit. We both wore plaster dust in our hair for weeks after we took down the fireplace brick by brick. We spent nights in bed talking about our plans for the house, the color of the walls, the design of the kitchen floor, the drapes in the dining room. I hated the thought of living anywhere else. I worried about leaving behind the one thing that gave Danny and me joy and a new focus as a couple, the strong, tall bond between us that I was reminded of every day when I pulled into the driveway.

But Joey, our son, needed us to move him forward as quickly and as responsibly as we could, to take full ownership of his welfare. I asked myself, if we stayed in our home, ten years later what would I say? *Yes, it is unfortunate that Joey never made it out of that special needs class, but look at the beautiful home we have!* I had to trust my instinct. I knew in my heart, and my head, that Joey needed an integrated preschool and needed it now. My family, including the babysitters, was willing to travel within reason, so I set out with Joey's needs inventory to look at the programs offered in surrounding towns.

Researching and visiting schools became a second job for me. I looked at thirteen in all—along the South Shore, on Cape Cod, and in the smaller towns around us. Striving for the ideal environment, one Joey would be comfortable in and where he could flourish, I found a program in Cohasset that met 80 percent of Joey's needs. It served the three towns of Cohasset, Scituate, and Hingham. It was an all-day, year-round program, and the teachers and the environment were calming, structured, and very visual. I was concerned by the high teacher-to-child ratio, and I felt that the large group of children in the classroom might startle Joey. However, the program met the majority of Joey's needs inventory; it ranked the highest out of the thirteen programs I had observed. In addition, July had arrived, and most programs started new students the last week of August, so we needed to sell our house and find a new one in short order. We listed our home with a local real estate agent. Joey played with the For Sale sign for hours, giving us time to pack.

Within two weeks, we decided to rent in Scituate, the least expensive town of the three. The real estate agent hadn't shown our house once and warned us that the real estate market was soft. With moving day just seventy-two hours away, a colleague approached me and asked if I had looked at the Project Grow program in Marion. Marion was the next town over, and Project Grow had classrooms in Marion, Mattapoisett, and Rochester. I had looked at the one in Mattapoisett. I loved the structure, the small class size, and the low teacher/aid-to-child ratio—one to two, better than on Joey's needs inventory. The Mattapoisett lead teacher, however, possessed an abrupt and curt demeanor, and, being attentive to and aware of Joey's needs, I knew her sharpness would make him uncomfortable. My colleague informed me that the most experienced pilot teacher of Project Grow, Robin Wilson, ran the Marion classroom. We hadn't moved yet, so I made an appointment to view the classroom, took out a clean needs inventory, and set out to look at number fourteen.

Robin Wilson stood about 5 feet 3, with short brown hair that gently outlined her empathetic face. Her voice, tender yet firm, commanded a structured and flourishing classroom. During the day, the children ate a snack and lunch right in the classroom. Occupational, physical, and speech therapists worked with the children as part of the structure of the day, also within the classroom. The integration ratio (special needs to normal functioning children) stood at six to six, an ideal mix.

Robin explained that every day she wrote in a home-to-school notebook, and I could write back with my concerns, questions, and accomplishments at home. The language-based program used picture boards as verbal cues with nonverbal children like Joey. The program ran from nine to one, Monday through Thursday, with a home visit on Friday. The staff did a few home visits before the program began, which Joey needed due to his difficulty in transitioning. The classroom and Robin Wilson were 95 percent the right fit for Joey, hands-down, the only drawback being that the program did not have a summer component. Because Joey would regress in the summer, the town had to provide a summer program for him or bear the cost of an outside one. Currently, the nearest one existed in Middleboro, about thirty miles away. I decided to figure out the summer piece later. Right then I had the perfect program for Joey a town away from our families, friends, and, most importantly, babysitters!

We canceled our rental in Scituate and replaced it with a rental in Marion. Keeping within our budget, we looked at the only property available at this late date, a supposedly renovated summer cottage. From the outside, the house looked small, but it veered off like a maze in random directions, outlining the landlord's arbitrary thought patterns direction adding on. I felt nauseated as the real estate agent, armed with a can of Lysol, showed us around, each room worse than the one before. The closet-size family room featured bright orange, wall-to-wall shag carpeting that squished when you walked on it, though it was dry to the touch. Everything reeked of mold and must, and based on the drafty rooms and the rattling windows, clearly the landlord had winterized the cottage by himself. I tried to stay focused on our objective—Joey's education and development.

During August we moved in slowly. I brought a few things over with Joey so he could begin to transition to this new environment. We had to appear moved in prior to the first home visit. I began painting rooms, organizing closets, arranging furniture, and doing anything else I could do to make it feel like our new life would be okay. My husband remained at the other house until we were completely moved into the cottage, still processing the ordeal taking place around him.

The home visits came and went, and I went to the Project Grow classroom for a visit with Joey the day before the program started. Joey clung to me the entire time, street signs in hand and pacifier in mouth. Every movement, sound, smell, and sight seemed to unnerve him, and I couldn't imagine him being able to function there the following day on his own. My eyes couldn't hide my thoughts, and Robin quickly sent a consoling glance in my direction.

The first day came. Robin, as well as the other teachers, came to our cars and took the children out of their car seats and into the classroom. Joey screeched in fear, though armed with his street signs and pacifier. Robin welcomed any items that brought the children comfort, though at that moment they provided little, if any, relief. I cried the ten minutes it took me to get back to the rental. The landlord, there to fix another leak, yelled hello when I entered, but I couldn't answer.

I turned around and got back in the car. I drove back to the old house, got out, and walked around. I went inside, looked around, and thought about all the plans and dreams we had made. When Danny first told me he had bought this house, I had cried. I hated it.

Twenty years before, when I was nine, my siblings and I had all packed into Mom's Pontiac Bonneville, and the brakes gave way. We drove right into this very yard and hit a rosebush. The two old women who lived in the house invited us in. The entire house smelled like onions. I remember it being dark and creepy, and the two women being eerie as well.

Restored, the house became bright and light and smelled of promise and success. This day it seemed a little darker, empty, and cold. I got back in the car, drove, and sobbed for two more hours until I ran low on gas on all fronts and ended up back at the rental.

What had I done? I had uprooted my family, taken my husband away from a home he loved, put Joey in a classroom with strangers in a strange town, and rented a soggy, wretched orange house. I felt so alone. I needed desperately for someone to tell me I had done the right thing—someone to tell me to trust my decision, my instinct, my gut. But the only person there clanged on the pipes so loudly that I barely heard the phone ring.

"Hello."

"Hi Anne. It's Robin. Robin Wilson."

My heart sunk. "Is everything okay?"

"Yes, Joey is doing great, and to show you how well he is doing, I am videotaping his entire day for you so you can watch it this afternoon. We'll videotape him often so you can feel confident in your decision and be part of his progress."

"Robin, I . . ." The tears wouldn't let me get the words out.

"I know. You don't have to say it; I saw it in your eyes. We can do this for him together. You're not alone. I have to get back to the classroom now, but I'll see you at pickup."

"Thanks."

I hung up the phone, sobbing and wet and relieved and happy, looking around for a tissue, anything. The landlord came from around the corner and handed me a clean rag. "My wife gets like that too, at least once a month." Letting out a big chuckle, I picked up a paintbrush and began painting Joey's new playroom.

Your Exercises

I am a creature of habit. I hate change. Joey's diagnosis not only forced him to step out of his comfort zone on many occasions, it also forced me to step out of mine. Adapting was difficult for me, yet I truly believe that had I not adapted quickly and moved Joey forward, his outcome would not have been as successful. I want you to take a minute and say "adapt" to yourself and really think about the definition: "to put oneself in harmony with changed circumstances." That is all you have been handed—changed circumstances. How you as a parent choose to deal with those changed circumstances will directly affect your child's outcome.

Tips

- *Begin the next step.* Now that you have gone through the exercise in Step Three and are beginning to realize how your acceptance can have a positive effect on your child's outcome and life, put that acceptance to the test with the next step: You must successfully adapt to the change.
- *Be flexible.* The process of adapting, as developed by Dr. Michael O'Connor, coauthor of *The Platinum Rule* (Warner Books, 1996), is one that requires flexibility. Flexibility is your willingness to adapt. Flexibility requires confidence, tolerance, compassion, optimism, and respect for others.[8] Increasing your confidence relative to your child's diagnosis is one way you can increase your flexibility.
- *Learn where you can be more flexible in your life.* This will help you adapt and put yourself in harmony with life's changes.

Exercises

Complete the exercises below and learn how to improve your ability to adapt.

A.   Confidence, the first attribute in flexibility, means that you believe in yourself; you trust your judgment and resourcefulness. List ten ways you can increase your confidence relative to your child's diagnosis. Include ways to educate yourself and others about your child's needs. Example: "I can increase my confidence by reading *Step Ahead of Autism*, thus gaining the knowledge, skills, and tools to provide myself and my child with a positive outcome."

1. _____

2. _____

3. _____

4. _____

5. _____

6. _____

7. _____

8. _____

9. _____

10. _____

B.   The second flexibility attribute is tolerance, or being open to accepting routines, habits, systems, and opinions different from your own. Write about an opportunity you took to be more tolerant so that you could provide a positive outcome for your child. The example can be as minor as allowing your child to have his favorite toy at the dinner table for comfort and a positive dinner experience. If you can't think of anything, consider what you could do to be more tolerant.

_____

_____

Write about an opportunity to be more tolerant that you did not take advantage of and share how it provided an unchanged or negative outcome.

_____

_____

How could being more tolerant have made the above experience better?

_____

_____

C.   The third part of flexibility is empathy and compassion. Empathy results in feeling the pain, confusion, frustration, and joy of your child. It is not pity or sympathy; it is much deeper. It says, "I can feel what it must be like to be you." It comes from the heart. Compassion is a deep awareness of the suffering of another coupled with the wish to relieve it.

Regarding Step B, write down what you think your child was feeling when you were being tolerant:

_____

_____

Write down what you think your child was feeling when you were being rigid:

_____

_____

Take a moment to reflect on these feelings:

_____

_____

_____

D. The fourth flexibility attribute is optimism. An optimistic atti-tude leads to a positive outcome. You have heard about the power of posi-tive thinking. If you think positively and are optimistic about your child's future, he will have a positive outcome. Optimism is contagious. Daily, for the next ten days, write down one positive detail. It can be as minor as, "My son smiled today." It doesn't matter if he didn't smile at someone or some-thing; he smiled and that is a positive detail.

Positive, hopeful details:

1. _____

2. _____

3. _____

4. _____

5. _____

6. _____

7. _____

8. _____

9. _____

10. _____

E.   The last flexibility characteristic is respect for others. This is the sincere desire to understand and consider other people's choices, commitments, and needs in relation to yours. This trait is important, as you will constantly need to balance your intuition about your child's needs and about how to best meet those needs while considering and understanding other people's opinions. Forming positive relationships with your child's doctors, educators, caregivers, and counselors is key to providing a positive outcome for your child. If the doors of communication between you and others are closed, your child's progress will be stunted. Working collaboratively with all parties does not mean you have to constantly give in to others' opinions but rather take them all into consideration, knowing that in the end, as the authority on your child, you will have the final say as to what direction is best.[8]

Step Six:
ADVOCATE

/Advocate/ **To plead in favor of**

I signed my name in the visitor log, grabbed a name tag, and clipped it to my coat. Two months into Project Grow, I sat anxious to hear what the team had to say about Joey's progress.

Sitting in the hallway, I felt confident about our school choice for Joey, impressed that the staff took time out to meet with us beyond the weekly communication I currently had with Joey's teacher, Robin Wilson.

"They're ready for you, Mrs. Burnett," Mrs. Watkins, the school secretary, announced.

"They're ready for me?"

I grabbed my coffee and walked toward Joey's classroom.

"Mrs. Burnett?"

"Yes?"

"The meeting is in the conference room across the hall." Mrs. Watkins signaled me with her folded reading glasses to a closed door adjacent to the waiting area.

Uncertain as to whether I could bring in my coffee cup, I lifted it in the air. Mrs. Watkins responded with an affirmative nod.

I backtracked down the hall, concerned now with my gym-bound attire. My choice of clothing seemed appropriate earlier in the day, when I assumed I'd be in the classroom, surrounded by flying finger paints and sticky Rice Krispies treats.

I opened the door slowly, seven pairs of eyes on me. A large brown oval conference table filled the room, barely housing the seven people who sat around it—most of whom I didn't know.

"Mrs. Burnett, I'm Marlene Hudson, the principal here at Sippican Elementary. Please take a seat." Marlene stood 5 feet 4 inches and had a full head of light brown wiry hair that sat just above her ears. She bounced around smiling and giggling nervously—reminding me of a bobble head character, her round head continuously swinging back and forth.

I sat down in the only seat available, sandwiched between Marlene and a young woman I didn't recognize. Inconspicuously, I tried to take in the entourage of people congregated around me—some still finishing their conversations, some making notes, some fixated on my attire, others on my coffee. The woman next to me slid a clipboard between my arms as she simultaneously pushed a small box of tissues to my end of the table.

"Look for your name and sign next to it to verify you were in attendance today."

To verify I'm in attendance? I looked down at the lengthy list of names until I found mine and signed next to it. I noticed Danny's name listed in a separate box below me. Was he supposed to come? Feeling I had entered the wrong room, I fixated my eyes on Robin Wilson, hoping to get her attention.

"If you aren't expecting any other attendees, Mrs. Burnett, I think we can begin."

Expecting other attendees? Who would I be expecting? I don't even know what I'm attending! I thought how strange and secretive this meeting felt, briefly reminding me of the mystery rides my parents used to take us on. Sometimes we would end up at the library, a museum, a playground, or at an ice cream stand. The mystery destination was always a fun or interesting place. One day, however, they brought us to a big hall. Elderly women dressed in white coats and missionary black shoes were passing out tiny cups of tasteless clear liquid.

"Grab a drink and then we'll go for ice cream," my mom said. My older sister Libby marched forward, focusing on the ice cream, never questioning a thing, and sucked down the potion. Not me, only five years old at the time. I refused to put any strange drink—especially served by nuns in white coats—into my mouth. I demanded more information. My mother finally revealed the secret—a liquid vaccine for polio. Clearly, she had planned this "mystery destination" well in advance. I drank the vaccine but refused the ice cream, irritated with the deception.

Right now I'd drink anything, served by anyone, if it granted my escape from this conference room.

"Let's get started," a large woman at one end of the table stated. "I'm Toni Horne, director of special needs for the Old Rochester Regional School District, which includes Sippican Elementary. You know Robin Wilson. Robin smiled.

Jumping in, the woman next to Robin introduced herself, "I'm Louise Silva, Joey's speech therapist."

"Carl Thompson, adjustment counselor and school psychologist."

"Sarah Johnson, director of Project Grow."

"Marlene."

"Amanda Stewart, occupational therapist."

"Robin Wilson will read over the individualized education plan [IEP] we've drafted for Joey, and if it meets your approval, you can sign the parent acceptance statement, and we'll get a final copy off to you," Toni explained as she passed down a copy of the plan to me. The plan, fifteen pages long, overwhelmed me. The first two pages told me my rights:

> You have the right to accept or reject the proposed IEP in whole or in part and a right to meet with school representatives to discuss the IEP within thirty days of the date of this notice. You have a right to request mediation or a due process hearing if you dispute a portion of the IEP.

A right to a hearing? I felt a pit in my stomach and wished I wasn't alone.

Robin continued reading the draft of Joey's IEP, which cited the goals, objectives, and methods they had determined for him:

> Joey exhibits delays in expressive and receptive language and social/communication skills. Joey reacts best to a consistent, predictable routine. Joey's parents are extremely supportive. Joey receives follow-up

evaluations at Children's Hospital in Boston, since his initial assessment.

Goal #1: Joey will increase his auditory processing abilities to develop his expressive and receptive language skills.

Objectives: Joey will demonstrate his understanding of following directions 60% of the time.

Method: Strategies that Joey will learn:

- Visualization (visual imagery)
- Chunking (remembering pieces)
- Self-questioning

Everyone mumbled to each other each time Robin read off a goal. I sat silent. "Mrs. Burnett, if you agree with the first goal, I will continue." I nodded, and Robin continued reading off the goals, all eight of them.

"Is there anything you challenge or would like to see omitted from the plan, Mrs. Burnett?" Toni Horne asked.

"Or is there anything you would like to add," suggested Robin. I couldn't speak. I barely understood the goals as they were read to me.

"If there are no changes, I can have Mrs. Watkins print off a fresh copy, and you could sign your acceptance right now," Toni Horne urged as she handed me a pen. Toni's physique, tall and broad, lent to a gentle giant's presence, like a bodyguard, a protector. Her face wide and undefined, she had a soft voice that people stopped and listened to, their reaction like a dog to a canine whistle.

Innately, I knew not to sign any official document without someone else looking at it. I also wondered why there weren't any goals made for Joey's social and emotional needs. Though language clearly remained his most obvious deficit, his social skills were just as absent.

"I'd like to take the plan home and give Danny an opportunity to look it over."

"Absolutely," the once-silent group around the table sang out in unison, Marlene with her head bopping about. "I'm also concerned that Joey's other needs weren't addressed."

"Other needs?" Toni Horne questioned.

"Yes," I cracked, clearing the intimidation from my throat. "Joey needs help with transitions—when the class goes to the library or out to the playground. And he needs someone to show him how to play with others or to indicate to an adult that he needs help. And what will happen when there is a fire drill. Joey . . ."

"Mrs. Burnett," Carl Thompson said, cutting me off. "Joey is an adorable little boy, and the few times I've observed him in the classroom and on the playground, he seemed fine with the other children." A tall handsome black man, Mr. Thompson talked in a soothing tone, his voice—cool and icy—gave me goose bumps.

"The few times you've observed him? The few times I have volunteered in the classroom, Robin Wilson has led Joey to the playground with a chain of pictures—door, hall, door, grass, swings, slide—and back to the door picture. Shouldn't this be addressed in Joey's plan? Isn't this something we want Joey to get better at—to require fewer pictures?" I could feel the goose bumps run up my back and the hair on my neck now standing at attention.

"I suggest you take the plan home, review it, and we meet again in a day or two," Toni said, her condescending voice now resonating through me. "Does that work with everyone's schedule?" I could feel my eyes swell. Amanda Stewart, the young women next to me, stated that she'd be unable to attend, but everyone else was available. "Mrs. Burnett, can you meet on Thursday, let's say 10:00 a.m.?"

A tear ran down my cheek as I reached for a tissue. "Yes, I can meet."

My hands now sweaty, I knocked over my coffee cup, spilling a little on the table. Robin left to retrieve paper towels as the others filed out of the room.

Nancy, an aide from another classroom, came in with a paper towel and wiped up the spilled coffee. "Tough meeting?" she asked, noticing the tissue clenched in my fist.

"I don't get it. Everyone knows what Joey's needs are . . . you know, you see him on the playground sometimes, right?"

Nancy shook her head.

"Why do I have to go over them again, go over the needs assessment again. They have a copy of it. I felt like I was being held on trial."

"They're just doing their job."

"What's their job, to intimidate me?"

"Think of their job as the opposite of dealing with a salesperson."

"Huh?"

"You know when you go to buy a car. They start at the base price and then want you to add a moonroof, air-conditioning, luggage racks—the whole nine yards?

"Yes?"

"Well, this is more like a food pantry. They want you to walk in and just take the bare minimum you can survive on—so there's leftover food, or in this case leftover budget money, for everyone."

"Am I supposed to feel guilty if I ask for what my child is entitled to and needs?"

"Absolutely not—the more special needs children in the school, the bigger the budget. You just have to be smart and thorough about what you ask for. You have to advocate for Joey."

"Advocate . . . you mean like a lawyer?"

"Like a mom. A mom who knows what Joey needs, without the tears." I tucked the tissue deep into my pocket.

"Don't get me wrong. I'd cry too if it were my child. It's so hard to keep the emotion out of the equation when you are talking about your child, someone you love and who can't speak up for himself. I'd be a mess. But this is a job for them, and they are professionals about it. They respond better to parents who are professional right back. They understand that language. They don't do well with tears; they don't know how to deal."

Nancy went back to her classroom, and I went back to Mrs. Watkins' desk to return the visitor tag, like a wounded police officer turning in my badge for crying on the job.

Later that afternoon, after a long walk, I pulled out Joey's diagnosis and needs assessment. I also looked online and researched parents' rights in Massachusetts, along with what types of therapies worked best for improving an autistic child's social and emotional needs. His needs assessment had already indicated some ways to help Joey improve:

> Representational and pretend play skills should be encouraged in an effort to foster Joey's lack of imagination. These activities should be enjoyable for all participants. A favored stuffed animal can be included in everyday activities, such as eating, dressing, and so on. Joey's favorite toys can be brought to the classroom at special times. Adults can respond to Joey's play and comment and model slightly more elaborate forms of

play with him. These are excellent tools to help him develop auditory attention and direction following. These activities have the additional advantage of providing enjoyable adult–child interaction.

The next day I perused libraries and bookstores. I realized that I needed more than one day to get my thoughts around Joey's plan and to write down the additional accommodations he needed. I also learned that I should have been given the plan at least one week prior to the meeting to have had ample time to review it. I learned I had the right to invite an advocate, one of Joey's doctors, or even a relative to the meeting, in addition to Danny.

Armed with this new information, I called the school and asked for Toni Horne, hoping to reschedule Thursday's meeting.

"Good morning, Sippican School. Mrs. Watkins speaking."

"Hi Mrs. Watkins. It's Anne Burnett. How are you?"

"I'm fine, Mrs. Burnett. How can I help you today?"

"I was hoping to speak to Toni Horne."

"Ms. Horne is out of the school at a districtwide meeting all day. Can I put you into her voice mail?"

"I wanted to reschedule tomorrow's meeting. Can you do that for me?"

"You have to put your request in writing, stating the reasons why. Normally they want forty-eight hours' notice, but since Toni Horne is unavailable, I will accept the letter, as long as you can have it to me by 1:00 p.m. today."

"Okay, fine. I'll bring it down by one."

I hung up the phone, angered by this time-wasting system. Meanwhile, Joey had been in Project Grow for two months, with no focus on his needs except for language. I took a deep breath and rubbed my eyes. No tears.

After four attempts and a half box of tissues, I composed the letter of a fighter, not a crier—and certainly not a quitter. The game was on.

November 7, 1993

Toni Horne, M. Ed.
Sippican Elementary
16 Spring Street
Marion, MA 02738

RE: Joey Burnett

Dear Ms. Horne:

This is to formally advise you that I am requesting a postponement of Thursday's meeting in regard to Joey's IEP. At a minimum, I am concerned that I never saw Joey's plan until it was placed in front of me at Monday's meeting, only two days ago, giving me little time to digest the plan, never mind challenge it, which wasn't my intent.

Joey needs more support than what he is receiving under his current IEP.

Clearly, you can imagine my amazement that not only do you and your colleagues feel he doesn't require any additional supports around his emotional and social needs but that his current IEP doesn't mention them anywhere.

I would like to point out that Danny and I spent over $400.00 in co-pays last summer in order that Joey receive out-patient social-skill services and ABA therapy through Beacon Services twice per week inasmuch as he was evaluated by their team as grossly inadequate in all sensory, emotional, and social skills. Theresa Johnson, who led the team at Beacon, went on to state that Joey uses hand-flapping and rigidity to compensate for his inabilities and he will continue to do so as he gets older and becomes more aware of the same.

I want to be clear that I am not dismissing the IEP in its entirety. However, as his doctors and therapists have all concurred, as Joey becomes more aware of his disabilities and social demands increase along with more transitions, he will grow more anxious and be less able to focus. I would assume you, as well as your colleagues, would trust the judgment of such astute medical professionals.

I will notify you within the next few days as to the dates I will be ready to reconvene so that we may redraft his IEP. In the meantime, I am enclosing Joey's needs assessment as prepared by Children's Hospital along with Beacon's progressive reports detailing Joey's progression last summer.

Sincerely,
Anne Burnett

Cc: Marlene Hudson, Principal
      Robin Wilson, Project Grow Teacher
      Carl Thompson, School Psychologist
      Amanda Stewart, O.T. Therapist
      Louise Silva, Speech Therapist
      Sarah Johnson, Director of Project Grow

I signed and delivered the letter to Mrs. Watkins, feeling proud of what I had composed. When I got home, I called the only family services agency in our area, two towns over, and asked if they had names of advocates in the area. The woman put me on hold, and after five minutes a young woman came on the phone.

"This is Lynn Bryant. Can I help you?"

"Hi Lynn. My name is Anne Burnett. I'm actually just looking to get a name of an advocate in the area."

"I can help you. I'm an advocate. How old is your child and where does he attend school?"

"Joey, my son, is three years old, and he attends Project Grow at Sippican Elementary School in Marion."

"Toni Horne's district. When can you meet?"

We scheduled a meeting for the next afternoon. Lynn asked me to bring any school correspondence I had, in addition to all Joey's assessments, diagnosis reports, and any other medical information I felt pertinent. I brought it all, in addition to my checkbook, as we never discussed cost.

Lynn had a freckled nose and straight blond hair to her shoulders. She was thin, almost frail looking, but her handshake was firm, and her eyes, almost a navy blue, were deep and soulful. She revealed that she had a son, John, age thirteen, who had Down syndrome, the reason she had become an advocate. Her services were free of charge and offered through a local nonprofit family services group. She instructed me to call the school and set up a meeting for a week from that day. Lynn also told me to tell them she was coming.

"You need to have your husband present too. Can he get the time off from work?"

As a salesperson for a mortgage company, Danny made his own hours.

"I'm sure he can make the time."

"Good. The more people present on our side, the better."

Suddenly, I felt as if I were at war, my son's future on the line. I felt my eyes fill up and I sniffed.

"We can do this. You have already made a case, right here, in these reports, assessments, and your checklists. Your son Joey will get what he needs, trust me."

I nodded.

"I want you to go home and over the weekend make a list of what additional services you feel Joey needs and why. Note what report backs your request. Make an extra set of your paperwork so you can mark it up. Let's meet back here on Tuesday morning at nine. Okay?"

"Sounds great, Lynn. Thanks so much."

We met Tuesday morning. I did exactly as Lynn had requested. I even wrote each service as a goal, similar to Joey's existing plan. I typed the list on my computer and made copies for Lynn and me. Lynn went over the goals I had listed and questioned the reasons behind each and every one of them. She asked me how we came to Project Grow and about Joey's history and birth. We met for more than two and a half hours. Drained and exhausted, I drove home mulling over what we had discussed. Lynn instructed me to wear a dress or skirt and Danny to wear business attire. We agreed to meet at the school fifteen minutes prior to our meeting on Thursday morning. I prepped Danny and explained the goals I wanted to add to Joey's plan.

Nervous and anxious, I didn't sleep at all Wednesday night. I took Joey to school and returned home to shower and put on a skirt and blouse from my banking days. Pulling on my jacket, I thought of the weekly board meetings I had conducted in this suit and wondered why now I couldn't speak up. I laughed to myself, thinking back to the day I had given my notice, with Joey just three months old. My boss, the president of Randolph Savings Bank, told me I'd be begging to come back within six months—I'd miss the challenges of the job too much.

Danny and I drove over together and met Lynn in the lobby. We signed in, took our badges, and sat in the hallway until they called our names. We entered the conference room, Marlene Hudson at one end and Toni at the other. One side of the table held Carl Thompson, Robin Wilson, and Louise Silva. The other side was empty. We filed into our seats and signed the clipboard sheet. Lynn knew everyone there, and they seemed pleased to see her, which I found comforting.

Robin Wilson began, reiterating my rights, then the goals on the existing plan. When Robin finished, Toni turned to me and asked for my concerns. I started, as Lynn had instructed me to, and read off my first additional goal for Joey: "Goal number nine: Joey will make gains in his personal and social development."

"That's a little open-ended. Can you be more specific?" I looked to Lynn to say something, but she didn't move.

"Well, I thought we could cover a lot of ground under this heading and break it down in the objectives for this goal. I've written a few," I gulped.

"Please, share."

"Objective: Joey will manage and adjust to transitions and/or changes without anxiety."

"Sounds good," Robin responded. She began typing on her laptop.

"Do you have a copy of the goals you want listed?" Toni asked.

I looked at Lynn to hand over her copy, but she didn't look up. She didn't do anything. Frustrated, I handed Toni my copy. She briefly looked it over and then looked around the table.

"The team will take these goals under consideration. Let's plan on meeting back here next week."

"No."

"I'm sorry?"

"No. We are not putting this off until next week," Lynn said, coming to life.

"Mr. and Mrs. Burnett have waited long enough to get Joey what he needs." She stood up and began walking around the edge of the room, forcing everyone to pull their chairs tighter to the table. "The Burnetts met with two separate teams of doctors at Boston Children's Hospital to obtain a diagnosis and an assessment for Joey, interviewed thirteen different schools, moved into a rental, and sold their beloved home so Joey could attend Project Grow, the preschool they believed would provide the best services, environment, and accommodations for their son. By extending their wait one more day, you are doing an incredible disservice, not only to them but to that little boy down the hall. The wait ends here and now. Let's roll up our sleeves and go over Mrs. Burnett's goals and objectives one by one until Joey's plan meets each and every one of his needs."

Robin grabbed the tissue box in the middle of the table, pulled out a tissue, and wiped her eyes. Clearing her throat, she began to speak: "I need to get back to the classroom, but I can work on the methods for all the objectives you come up with today."

Lynn thanked her and sat back down. Toni smiled at Lynn.

"Let's take a five-minute break, and I'll have my secretary make additional copies of your list of goals for Joey."

I thanked her. Everyone left the room except for Lynn, Danny, and me.

"Do you need me to stay, or can you take it from here?" Danny asked, his phone vibrating away.

"We'll be fine," Lynn chimed in.

"Thanks Lynn, for what you said, for what you did. I wanted to cry when you were talking about Joey and what we went through to this point, but I know I'm supposed to leave my emotions out."

"I disagree. Emotion got you here, and emotion will carry you through—never lose that. It's your passion for Joey that drives you. Your passion will fuel his success. Advocating is the by-product of all you feel for your family and want for your child. The administrators just needed to be reminded of the child and the family behind the plan."

By three o'clock that afternoon, Joey's plan was complete—fifteen goals and all the accommodations he'd ever need.

Your Exercises

Joey's first IEP meeting was the only meeting for which I engaged an advocate. I learned quickly how to funnel my passion into progress for Joey. I found my voice and fell into my role. As a parent, you bring very important information to the IEP meeting. Only you know your child's strengths and weaknesses and all the little differences that make your child unique.

Your knowledge can help the team develop an IEP that will work best for your child. Tell the team what goals are most important to you and to your child. You must speak up, share your concerns, and give insights about your child's interests, likes, dislikes, and learning style.

Sippican Elementary, Project Grow, Robin Wilson, and all the administrators were truly instrumental in providing Joey a successful integrated education. It was my role to show them what Joey needed and why, so we could work together collaboratively in providing him with a complete IEP.

Parents' Rights

The Individuals with Disabilities Education Act (IDEA), passed in 2004, ensures services to children with disabilities throughout the United States. IDEA governs how states and public agencies provide early intervention, special education, and related services to more than 6.5 million eligible infants, toddlers, children, and youth with disabilities.[9] To find the specific guidelines and requirements for your state, visit http://idea.ed.gov.

Tips

Once you have familiarized yourself with your rights, keep the following in mind when advocating for your child:

- *No one knows your child better than you.* Your recorded observations are the best source for diagnosing his condition.
- *You have the right to be respected and to make decisions for your child.* The best possible treatment for autism occurs with early diagnosis and intervention. Your records of how your child responds to stimuli should be the blueprint for a treatment plan.
- *You have the right to be heard.* You are more of an authority on your child than any professional caregiver. Your observations of your child are valid. As the primary caregiver of your child, you see things that might be overlooked in a diagnostic situation.
- *You have the right to request an evaluation of your child.* You also have

the right to be involved from start to finish if you suspect a developmental problem. Infants and toddlers through the age of two are eligible for care through early intervention programs. To qualify, your child must undergo a free evaluation.

- *Children over the age of three are eligible for assistance.* Check out school-based early intervention and special needs programs.
- *If your child's assessment reveals a developmental problem, you have the right to work with an intervention treatment provider.* Together you can create an individualized family service plan.
- *You have the right to invite those who know your child best to be on the IEP team.* This team might include family members, physicians, teachers, or others who understand your child's needs.
- *You have the right to disagree with the school system's recommendations and seek outside evaluation.* Free or low-cost legal representation is available if you cannot come to an agreement with school evaluators.[10]

Exercises

Below is a list of what to bring and what to consider prior to your child's IEP meeting. The key to a successful meeting is preparation. The more you know about your child's needs and about the IEP meeting, the better equipped you will be to ask questions, give feedback, and play an important role in the formation of your child's educational plan.

IEP Meeting Checklist

❏ Keep a folder or binder with all your child's assessments and medical records on one side, the most recent on top. On the other side, have lined loose-leaf paper. Keep a couple of pens and pencils tucked inside.

❏ Bring a water bottle and cough drops or hard candies. If you start coughing or get choked up, they will bring some comfort and will serve as a distraction.

❏ If it is your child's second meeting or beyond, make sure you have copies of previous plans and progress reports with you so you can compare them.

❑ If it is your first meeting, educate yourself prior to the meeting. Go online, to the library, or to your local bookstore to read up on IEPs and become familiar with their format. Ask the school secretary for a blank IEP form if you can't find one online.
❑ Make a list of therapies your child has received since birth.
❑ Make a list of routines, toys, and rituals that work at home, and make a list of what doesn't work.
❑ Make a list of any issues your child will have around snack or lunchtime.

What to Consider
Bring a list of concerns and any noteworthy behaviors you are witnessing at home, to your child's IEP meeting.

1. Do you have any needs or concerns if your child takes the school bus to and from school?
2. Does your child need to take breaks often or have sensory issues?
3. Is your child prone to distractions?
4. How will the school handle transitions?
5. Does your child have issues with fine or gross motor skills?
6. Does your child have toileting needs?
7. Does he take medication?
8. Does she require a full-time aide?
9. Does he have hearing or vision problems?

Below, list concerns that are not covered on the prescreening checklist or on your child's needs assessment. Example: "My son is fearful of candles. We need to incorporate a strategy for him if birthdays are celebrated in the classroom."

1. _____

2. _____

3. _____

Step Seven:
ASSESS YOUR ATTITUDE

/Assess Your Attitude/ **To determine the importance, size, or value of a mental, emotional, or physical position toward a fact or state**

The conversation was all it could be at 4:30 a.m. The driver, a long-distance acquaintance of my mother, was a rail-thin, rough-edged, short-haired woman in her late sixties. Her salt-air-weathered skin hosted deep terrains on her road-mapped face—from a love of sailing, she'd tell you, though rumor and the owner of the local spirits store talked more of her love of drink. Jane looked me over with an obvious gaze of pity while, using all my strength, I pulled myself up into her oversize commuter van.

Alone in the dark, with a mere stranger driving me to Faulkner Hospital in Jamaica Plain on the western side of Boston, to undergo surgery on something as personal and private as my ovaries, I could see in her eyes that she longed to split a few tales and a few tall ones with me. I barely had enough energy to muster up a "Good morning."

She didn't know I'd chosen this plan. I didn't choose to have surgery to remove acute endometriosis—life just throws you curves sometimes—but I did choose to have someone other than Danny or another family member drive me in. Joey would panic without Danny or me to greet him and to keep his routine when he woke up in the morning. My family had already done so much for us, and honestly, the drive up could have been with anybody as I, half-asleep and half-empty after ingesting "cleansing" medication the night before, just craved sleep.

Dozing on the way up, partly to avoid chatting with Captain Rye and partly to take my thoughts away from what was to come, my mind drifted back to my first surgery.

I had moved back home, at twenty-one years old, a week before my father was diagnosed with terminal lung cancer and on the same day my sister Libby had come home from her jaunt across Portugal pregnant and husbandless. I wondered which circumstance was more difficult to comprehend for my diehard Irish Catholic mother, though sadly, secretly, I knew.

To watch a human life deteriorate and waste away a little bit every day, as you stand by helplessly—a life that you looked to for strength, direction, comfort, judgment, acceptance, and approval—is like no other form of torture. Dad was my anchor in life, and now I felt as if I were drifting with no direction, no land in sight. Being the youngest, I recall my childhood quite differently than the others. Where my father failed my older siblings, he inspired me, proud of my accomplishments and dismissive of my shortcomings. Our relationship was one of mutual respect. We talked at the dinner table, long after the dishes had been cleared, about his dreams as a young man and my creative ideas for the future. He had a gift for motivating people.

A long white picket fence ran along the side of our property. One summer, when I was eleven years old, it was my turn to help paint the fence, as my five older siblings had already done their share of fence painting. Every morning I would get up, have breakfast, and go out to tackle the fence, but the job never seemed to be done. Finally I complained to my father and said, "Dad, I still have so far to go. I'll never get the fence painted." My dad looked right at me with a big smile and replied, "Yes, but look at how far you've come." I turned around and more than three-quarters of the fence was painted. I was so focused on getting the job done that I hadn't looked at what I had accomplished to that point.

Then, eleven years later, having him decline before me was more than I could digest. I assumed the pains in my lower abdomen were a byproduct of my grief. My father, an optometrist in town, occupied an office adjacent to my gynecologist, Dr. Cooney. During my appointments, Dr. Cooney and I would console each other; he'd prescribe pain medicine for me, and I would update him on my father's prognosis.

My father passed away in February, and my sister gave birth in May, but my abdominal pain never subsided. One Saturday in June, I was upstairs in my mother's home, alone, the pain intolerable. Going downstairs to get to the phone, I tripped and went headfirst down the steps and landed on my stomach. Unable to stand up, I crawled to the phone and called Dr. Cooney at his home. He arrived within minutes. He gave me a shot for the pain and operated two days later, removing orange-size cysts created by my newly discovered and severe case of endometriosis.

Jane and I arrived at Faulkner in time for my pre-op and blood work, about 6:30 a.m. I stood on the sidewalk and watched Jane drive away. I should have told her about Joey, I thought. She'll probably tell everyone in town that my own family wouldn't drive me to surgery. Deciding I didn't care, I made my way to the pre-op floor.

My doctor estimated that the surgery would take no longer than an hour and a half. It took five hours, my body feeling every second of it. In the recovery room, I could hear the nurses talking around me, but I couldn't get their attention. I felt like I was yelling, but the words weren't audible. Aching to be heard, I thought how frustrating it must be for Joey, and I wished I were home.

My doctor came by at 4:00 p.m. to check on me and tell me of the successful surgery, setting my discharge time around 6:00 p.m., once I had walked around and could breathe without the aid of an oxygen tube up my nose. But miscommunication between my doctor and the nurses' station actually put my discharge time at 8:00 p.m. Danny arrived at 9:30 p.m. to take me home, frustrated by the time of night and the long ride before us. Exhausted and in pain, I ignored his mood.

We arrived home. My mother, babysitting Joey, made conversation as I slowly made my way to bed.

"Joey won't go to sleep until you read him his book. I'm so sorry. I tried," Mom confessed. I pulled myself up and made it to Joey's room, my mother guiding me along. Joey, anxious and edgy, sat on the edge of his bed, his face exhibiting more pain than I felt. I maneuvered myself up on to his bed, and he pulled out *Happy and Sad, Grouchy and Glad* from under his pillow. Mom whispered good-bye, and I read, "'I'm feeling sad today,' Grover cried."

Back safely in his routine, Joey sluggishly turned the page, bedtime now making sense to him. Asleep before I could finish the book, he hugged his pillow and I tucked him in. I cautiously made my way to bed, Danny already asleep.

Pain pills yet to kick in, I lay there thinking about the day—the isolated ride up, the lengthy surgery, and the solitary ride home. I thought about the morning I had helped my brother take down my dad's hospital bed after he died and how I casually looked out his bedroom window, only to witness the medical examiners carrying him away in a body bag. My inspiration, my anchor—my dad—being carried off like clothes being delivered to a rummage sale. I longed to hold Joey. Wet faced and sore, I stumbled to his room, kissed his forehead, and silently promised him a painted fence.

Your Exercises

A positive attitude enables you to look at what appears to be an impossible situation and find alternative ways to make it work. When I realized I needed surgery, my family couldn't grasp how I could make it happen; Joey needed Danny and me, and I would be needy myself.

I approached the day with a positive opinion by focusing on Joey's needs first: providing him with a typical day by having Danny or me there to greet him in the morning and get him through the day, with the help of his favorite babysitter, my mom. My doctor agreed to schedule the surgery very early to ensure my departure the same day, though that part did not go as smoothly.

Many days don't go as we plan. Young children, especially autistic children, need a structured day. Although healthy young children focus on only their needs and fuss when those aren't attended to, autistic children suffer pain and discomfort when basic needs such as structure and routine are not met.

Undergoing five hours of surgery, enduring pain and exhaustion, I wanted to focus on my needs and just go to bed. Clearly I had reason to feel negative and irritable, but I chose the alternative. Joey needed closure to his day. Reading to him for barely ten minutes brought peace to Joey and true joy and strength to me. A positive, flexible attitude is something you need to possess and nurture throughout your child's life.

Tips

- *Start by tweaking.* With an open mind and a positive attitude, put the wheels in motion for improving your child's life by tweaking your attitude.
- *Run your ideas by people.* Go to those who are positive influences in your life, whether family members, teachers, friends, or colleagues.
- *Stay away from pessimists and negative thinkers.*
- *Engage in positive thoughts and communication.* Instead of "I can't" or "I won't," say "I can" and "I will." You'll be pleasantly surprised how often a positive approach brings positive results.

Exercises

Look at your child's life right now. Is there a minor issue that could be resolved or beneficially dealt with by changing your perspective—something related to your child's education, home life, or well-being?

1. Write down an aspect of your child's daily life that is causing you frustration or concern.

_____

_____

_____

2. Why is this aspect frustrating or concerning?

_____

_____

_____

3. List three things that can improve this situation, even if you feel they
    can't be accomplished.

    a. _____

    b. _____

    c. _____

4. Which of the three above do feel you could accomplish with help?

    _____

5. List three ways you could accomplish your answer to Question 4.

    a. _____

    b. _____

    c. _____

Example #1

Recently, the grandmother of Will, a three-year-old boy suspected of
autism and delayed speech, shared with me concerns about her grandson's
preschool problem:

> My daughter, Liz, is frustrated because she has no daily communica-
> tion with Will's teacher. With newborn twins at home, Liz is unable to
> take or pick up Will from school, times when the other parents have daily
> communication with the teacher. She has tried e-mailing and phoning the
> teacher, but it takes a few days for the teacher to get back to her. I have
> offered to go to work late and watch the twins so my daughter can meet
> the teacher, but Liz is too nervous to leave the twins yet. I feel so frustrated
> because there needs to be more communication. Liz feels frustrated with
> the school because many issues Will faces require daily interaction with
> his teacher.

The grandmother and her daughter felt frustrated with each other and the preschool. I suggested that the boy's mom call the school and ask the teacher to call her back when she was available to talk for at least ten minutes. I further suggested that when the teacher called back, the mom should offer to resolve the communication issue by providing her with a home-to-school notebook. In the notebook, the mom could write every day, detailing any concerns or accomplishments from the previous day, and the teacher could do the same.

Three weeks later the grandmother called to thank me for opening up the lines of communication between her and her daughter and between her daughter and the boy's teacher. A small change—a notebook—made a world of difference. All the parties involved were too frustrated to look beyond their own concerns, but all they needed to do was step back and take a positive approach to the problem.

Example #2

Joey's preschool, Project Grow, did not offer a summer component, something Joey truly needed. One option was for Joey to attend a school about thirty minutes away. Transitioning him into a new program for two months would be difficult. The first half of the school year, I conjured up negative thoughts and feelings about the summer school program, angry that the school system didn't offer one locally. Other parents told me that they too dreaded the drive and noontime pickup. In an ideal world, Joey would attend Project Grow all summer, with the same children, here in town.

I could have continued to harbor a poor attitude about the summer school situation, but instead I stepped back and asked myself, *What can I do?* I had been working at the local yacht club in town part-time while Joey was in class. I knew the club would be able to replace me over the summer, when many students were looking for work. I contacted Robin Wilson and shared my idea: I would offer a summer program at my house for six children, three normally functioning and three with development delays, Joey being one of them.

One of the teachers in Project Grow offered to run the program with me. The mothers, myself included, all chipped in a small stipend to pay the teacher and provide snacks. The parents took up a collection to pay me what I would have earned at the yacht club during the summer and presented the money to me on the last day of camp. The program was a huge success.

Step Eight:
ASSERT YOUR AUTHORITY

/Assert Your Authority/ **To state or declare positively and often forcefully or aggressively that you are the person in command**

Left side of the street, third space back—I tactically parked the car for school pickup, placement now an art form. Fall presented a challenge with new parents haphazardly parking everywhere. Two weeks before—forced to park five spaces back—I got out of my car and stood near the Honda Pilot occupying my sacred space, trying to keep some sense of routine for Joey. Retrieving a pen and paper out of my purse, I wrote down our license plate number. Street signs, license plates, exit numbers on highways—Joey memorized random data. He'd point out a replaced or updated street sign. He'd wave to passing cars when he recognized their license plates—friends and neighbors to me, numerals to him. Letters and numbers fueled his mental well-being and helped him make sense of his world.

Seeing Joey make his way in the distance, I knelt down next to the intrusive Honda Pilot and placed my makeshift number over its plate. Perched, I waved to Joey with one hand and pointed to the number with the other. He repeated the number to himself as he crossed the street. Once Joey was within reach, I grabbed his hand and showed him to our car. I thought I'd completed a successful mission, but the parking space issue left him anxious for weeks—would I be sure to get our space tomorrow? The next day? The day after that? I spent hours reassuring him—a promise I didn't intend to break.

Following the incident, I kept my vow and showed up twenty minutes early every day, protecting the space like a mother grizzly marking her den to ensure her cub finds his way home.

Today, securely parked, I watched from my car window as mothers began to cluster together, strategically placed along the front walk leading to Sippican Elementary School. Like Buckingham Palace foot guards, they took their posts twice daily—once at 8:00 a.m. and again at 3:00 p.m. Chatting while sipping the foam atop their caffe lattes, their cool breath swirled through the air.

Tucked in my den, I looked on and imagined what they chatted about—sales at the local stores; the latest case of strep throat; Ms. Duggan, the disorganized fourth-grade teacher, and Friday night's Harvest Hop.

Twice a year, spring and fall, the elementary school held a hop for the kids, orchestrated by the parents. The school supplied the deejay and gym, parents brought the cookies and punch. The kids ran around and screamed at the top of their lungs, crunching cookies as music blared in the background. The spring before I had volunteered to make cookies. I had planned to bring Joey with me to deliver the goodies. Fleeting thoughts suggesting our lives were normal occurred from time to time. This was one of them.

Taking a child with such a severe sensitivity to noise that he startled when the refrigerator came on in the next room to a gymnasium of one hundred–plus kids jumping and yelling to music being played at two hundred decibels was clearly an error in judgment. Five minutes into our bakery drop, Joey had a bloody nose from the pressure in his head. I pulled off my scarf, applied it to his face, and quickly made our escape before anyone noticed us.

The school bell rang, interrupting the moms' conversations. The front doors flung open. Kids piled out in droves. Those still young enough to run to their mothers' arms were met with a hug, followed by a toss in the air. Some children balanced corrected projects, posters, and experiments. Others appeared as if they had just been through a battle, their captive backpacks scraping the cement behind them. Famished children scrambled through their lunchboxes, gobbling up leftovers.

Joey, at the front of the pack, made his way down the center path and headed directly for the sidewalk, where he waited apprehensively for the crossing guard's instructions. Fran, a big-boned Swedish woman of sixty-two years, standing 5 feet 11, had been the crossing guard since we moved to Marion. Previously a state trooper, she appreciated Joey's need for order and precision and quickly learned his method for successfully crossing the street. Taking extra time to make sure the road was free and clear from all angles, Fran instructed him to cross with a wave of her white glove. Joey, his eyes painfully fixated on her, stepped down off the sidewalk vigilantly.

Fran had taken special notice of the collection of key rings dangling from Joey's backpack: two red stop signs, a railroad crossing gate, a street-light that flashed when you pressed a black button, a yellow pedestrian symbol, and his favorite, the Hunchback of Notre Dame—all of which swung in unison as he trudged along. Joey had been obsessed with Disney movies from eighteen months old. He'd watch only one movie over a long period—eight, twelve, sixteen months—and analyze each character's mannerisms, speech, and movements. I'd try to get him to watch different videos, shorter ones, other Disney movies—he wouldn't. Only he knew when he had scrutinized every movement, every word, gesture, and element. Only then would he move on to another Disney movie.

When he was in kindergarten five years earlier, Joey had chosen a backpack boasting Mickey Mouse and three princesses dancing in front of Cinderella's castle. As he walked up to the school door, captivated by the princesses on his shoulder, Joey remained thankfully oblivious as I fended off glares from other parents. Submerged in a sea of L. L. Bean–initialed backpacks, we were immediately branded different. This label that I tried at first to rub off, I now wore proudly—effectively—to our advantage.

Fran swayed to the clang of the key chains as Joey passed by. I think it fascinated her that he seemed not to notice the sound—or did he? Maybe the clang made sense to him, beating a rhythm, playing a tune that only he understood. At times I sensed that Joey operated on a different level, within a different layer of existence, and he selected people with whom to share that existence. These people got to see glimpses of his world. Fran became one of his chosen ones—a trusted soldier in his private war. She adored Joey and protected him as long as he was in her sight—her beat—and I felt thankful for that.

Since Joey appeared more nervous and anxious than usual, Fran said only a word or two to him, gently smiling at me as if we shared a secret. Mondays had become increasingly difficult for Joey, though I wasn't sure why. Now in fourth grade, Joey had made great strides academically. His expressive speech was grade level; his receptive speech six months behind. But social and emotional issues began to take a physical toll. It had become routine almost every Monday: Ridden with a migraine headache, he jumped in the car and I raced home. Most times we made it to the house before he threw up. Sometimes we made it to the driveway. Once we didn't get out of the parking space. We had the routine down now. Exhausted by the ordeal, he would go upstairs and sleep for an hour. It depleted him and pained me to watch. The other days his headaches were not as severe.

As fourth grade marched on, the headaches seemed to get worse and more frequent. I talked to the school psychologist, Carl Thompson, and asked if Joey displayed agitation or frustration more frequently than usual. I asked if Joey made friends and socialized with others, either in the lunchroom or on the playground. Thompson insisted that Joey seemed fine. He continued to discuss the academic gains Joey had made. Joey, orderly and with almost savantlike intelligence, made it easy for his superiors to ignore his obsessive-compulsive behaviors and lack of social cues.

Hopeful that school wasn't the source of Joey's headaches, I made an appointment with a neurologist at Massachusetts General Hospital, Dr. Hanlon, a Harvard graduate. Joey's pediatrician had warned me of Dr. Hanlon's cold bedside manner, a "normal" personality trait of many neuro-anythings. But his residency at Boston Children's Hospital and his specialty in working with children on the autism spectrum made him seem warm and fuzzy to me. He saw patients at Mass General in Boston and at his satellite office in Plymouth. I chose Plymouth for the initial consult, knowing that we could go to Boston for further testing.

Looking a bit like the late John F. Kennedy Jr.—tall and thin with dark hair and bleached white teeth—he was physically stunning, but his voice, dry and clinical, made me sleepy. For the first twenty minutes, Dr. Hanlon checked Joey's vision, balance, coordination, and reflexes while asking me questions about his symptoms. He asked Joey to lift up his shirt, and as he checked under his arms, my heart sank. Lumps?

He pulled down the shirt and asked me about Joey's previous school year, third grade, seeking differences between this year and the one before.

The only difference was Ms. Duggan, his teacher. She was disorganized and difficult for Joey to take direction from. Though Joey's special needs aide had remained constant since kindergarten, his teachers had not. At times I thought Ms. Duggan was intimidated by Joey's obsessive organization, logic, and exactness. Once she had called Danny and me in for a parent conference to tell us that Joey was so intelligent that she couldn't keep him challenged, blaming her limited intellect on him. He'd correct her if she were one-sixteenth of a second late, a letter off, a lesson behind, or if she had forgotten to dot an i. Joey couldn't comprehend how everyone else wasn't exact, every day, all the time. To him we were the dysfunctional ones.

Dr. Hanlon reviewed Joey's history, which came from my ample supply of reports and tests. He commented as he read about each of Joey's struggles with smells, sounds, commotion, crowds, tactile defensiveness, and transitions. I explained that though these behaviors still existed, they now lay dormant, rearing their ugly heads only when he was overtired, sick, or pulled out of his routine.

"He is out of his routine," Dr. Hanlon announced.

"Today? I had to pull him out of school to see you," I said defensively.

"No. Joey's . . . no." Catching his tone, Dr. Hanlon stopped himself. "Joey has started puberty. Imagine a fire alarm going off inside your body."

I cringed.

"Now imagine a fire alarm going off inside of Joey."

I couldn't.

"Puberty amplifies sounds, smells, and crowded spaces, igniting behaviors. Joey, now verbal and academically flourishing, has innately developed strategies to 'handle' some behaviors. He chooses what materials feel good to him. Smells, however, he has no control over. No control—coupled with his obsessive need to be rule conscious—results in a headache and nausea. Joey endures the smells, the noisy hallways, and students talking out of turn in class until the end of the day, when he can physically, comfortably, safely release it."

"What can I do?"

"Change his environment. That would be the best scenario. However, I can prescribe anxiety medication and something for his headaches."

"What would you do if he were your son?"

Without hesitation Dr. Hanlon said, "I'd pull him," his voice cracking.

Driving home, Joey slept while I tried to process what "change his environment" would mean for Joey, me, our family. Sippican Elementary worked for him. It was the reason we had moved, plotted a new path, and changed our lives. And where would he go? I felt like I was at ground zero, back eight years to when I had first begun looking at schools. Complacency had silently crept into my being. My body ached. I turned up the radio and thought about teacher gifts I still needed to get for the last day of school the following Tuesday. Maybe Joey's last day at Sippican. Quietly, I cried the rest of the ride home.

Summer came and fourth grade ended, as did Joey's headaches, momentarily convincing me that he could finish out his elementary years at Sippican. Sippican Elementary hosted grades K–6 and Project Grow, the integrated preschool Joey had attended. Aside from me having to advocate for him year to year, month to month, week to week, the school worked. I understood Toni Horne and Joey's team, and I knew how to motivate them. Though Joey's challenges changed every year, the school had a system in place to help him and me.

The last day of summer camp brought the first day of headaches, mild but prevalent. On August 29, two weeks away, Sippican Elementary would resume classes. I knew I had to move quickly. The energy I didn't have at the end of fourth grade I made up for now. The thought of Joey having to endure headaches and nausea again delivered new strength. Subtly, during the summer, I dropped hints to Danny and my family. Sippican, with its now thirty-plus class sizes and noisy cafeteria, might not be the ideal location for Joey. I researched several schools within driving distance, including the Wheeler School on the east side of Providence, Rhode Island. The Wheeler School offered an on-campus program called Hamilton, which teaches learning-challenged children. One of its specialties is dyslexia. Joey, now high functioning academically, wouldn't have the tolerance for a multitude of learning and teaching styles. Additionally, the fifty-minute drive via carpool or bus would tax him.

Some of the children in town went to Friends Academy, a private school in Dartmouth, Massachusetts, about twenty-five minutes away. The academy didn't offer any special needs program and had a waiting list, but I had to research every option. I made an appointment with Linda Kelsey, the admissions director. On the phone she stated that Friends had one opening for a male entering fifth grade and two female openings for the fourth grade. Most children go straight through from kindergarten to eighth grade, rarely leaving an opening. A family relocation had created the three available slots.

Founded by Quakers in 1810, the school—housed in a fieldstone Tudor brandishing tall peaked roofs and medieval doors with black iron latches—is set back off windy Tucker Road on sixty-five acres. Ms. Kelsey met me in the school's foyer with a firm handshake and a packet of papers.

"I thought I'd take you on a tour and answer your questions as we walk along. We can go over the forms and your next steps when we're finished."

Not waiting for my acknowledgment, she began her speech. "This building accommodates grades one through six, while grades seven and eight are housed in a separate building in the rear."

Ms. Kelsey, with light brown hair and glimpses of blond, had huge brown eyes and dark brown eyelashes that provided striking contrast to her highlights. At a commanding height of 5 feet 9, dressed head to toe in Ralph Lauren, she reeked of academia and old wealth. I was sure she was quickly assessing me and the late time of year to be touring and gatherered that she was walking and talking swiftly with the goal of putting a speedy end to our tour. Focused on Joey's needs, I ignored her pompous air and pulled out a checklist I had compiled. Halfway through my checklist, Ms. Kelsey—seemingly impressed by my thorough interrogation—slowed down and divulged the real information I needed:

- No cafeteria.
- Children bring their own lunches and eat in the classrooms.
- Teachers rotate the seating at lunch, so students sit near someone new daily.
- Nine-student limit per classroom.
- No talking in the hallways and common areas.
- In every fifth-grade classroom, the desks are assembled in a horse-shoe; no one is in front or in back of the room.
- Minimum number of transitions.
- Recess consists of talking outside in a circle or a free study period.
- Intelligence is revered; the word nerd isn't in the student's vocabulary.

Noting I was pleased with my findings, Ms. Kelsey pointed out that Joey would still need to take an entrance exam and spend a day at Friends, something he wouldn't have the opportunity to do if he were to start Sippican the following week. Friends Academy started in two.

"Passing the entrance exam doesn't mean automatic acceptance; it stills needs to be the right fit for the school and for your son," Ms. Kelsey pointed out.

Knowing in my heart that Joey would thrive in this rule-conscious, no-talking, no-cafeteria circle of lunchtime friends, in this Disney-like castle, I scheduled the entrance exam for the next day. Heading home, I heard everyone's objections in my head: *You're pulling him for headaches. Did you even try the medication? Friends Academy doesn't offer special needs services. Joey's IEP will be dissolved. What if the headaches continue and he needs to throw up on the way home? You'll never make it now. We can't afford the tuition.*

Joey needed patience, acceptance, and social nurturing. Friends Academy offered all three. My goals for Joey had never been about academics. I wanted him to be able to speak and talk, yes, but so much more I wanted him to feel, laugh, cry, and be happy with himself and others. I remembered Dr. Brazelton's words years earlier: "If Joey is comfortable in his environment, he'll flourish."

Clearly, he wasn't comfortable at Sippican. I knew a small, supportive environment would provide the opportunity to strengthen his social skills and foster friendships. I believed Friends Academy to be the right placement for Joey and continually reiterated my reasons to family and friends.

Joey passed the exam and spent a day at Friends, its actual first day of school. Ms. Kelsey came out to the parking lot to meet us. I kissed Joey's forehead in front of the medieval door. The iron latch closed behind them. I prayed I had made the right decision. On the way home I drove down Spring Street, past Sippican Elementary. There, in the center of the road, was Fran, dear Fran. I hadn't remembered to tell her. I pulled over, got out of my car, and ran over to her.

"Fran, I am so sorry I didn't make a point of telling you the day school started. Joey's at Friends."

"I know. I heard. I have something for him," she said graciously.

She went to her car and came back with a key chain. It was round and green, with gold lettering that spelled out the word Maine. In the middle of the circle was a moose.

"Who needs the L. L. Bean backpack when you can have the real thing?" Fran said smiling. She was not only aware of Joey's struggles but surprisingly knew mine too. I hugged and thanked her.

"He'll be fine," she whispered, recognizing my uncertainty.

"I just wish I could be with him. I don't know anyone there."

"You're there with him in everything he does, watching over him from afar."

That afternoon, on the drive to pick up Joey from Friends, I thought about what Fran had said and realized she was right. I had made the best choice I possibly could as the authority on my child, and I needed to have faith in my decision.

Joey had a great first day, and within a week the headaches and nausea were gone—never to return.

Your Exercises

By definition, authority means the power to act on behalf of someone else or to be a reliable source of information on a subject. Three things that can negatively affect our authority are complacency, fear, and lack of motivation. I had been willing to invest the time and effort to ensure Joey was properly instructed at Sippican Elementary, and I felt content with the results. At some point, my contentment became complacency. It is critical for us as parents to recognize when that happens. I also felt fearful to make a change in Joey's life—a change that I knew would bring resistance from family and friends.

Example

Recently, at the end of one of my workshops on advocacy, a woman in her mid-fifties approached me about her eighteen-year-old son. He had been diagnosed with Asperger's syndrome at the age of three. The woman had always been a single mom and spent much of her life advocating for him. She said he was graduating from high school that spring and would enter a transitional school that taught life skills and took the students to a small mall twice per week to visit the stores. The woman stated that though her son was low functioning and still didn't understand social skills, the transitional school wouldn't be challenging enough for him. Instead of having him visit the mall, she preferred that he be introduced to responsibilities, such as working at something that he enjoyed to build his confidence and independence.

I tried to get a clearer understanding of her son's abilities, but almost every other word out of her mouth was negative, pointing out her son's weaknesses and all she had done for him on her own. I asked if she had received any respite. She stated that the amount she received from the state was a joke, again focusing on the negative. At this point I decided to focus on her son's experience at high school. Her face lightened up. She talked nonstop about how much she loved the school system her son had attended for the previous fifteen years. "I think I'm going to miss his teachers more than he will," she confessed. I realized that the negativity I had heard in her voice at the beginning of our conversation was fear. The future frightened her. She needed to replace her fear with motivation and assert her authority to get a better plan in place for her son. I began by asking what her son liked to do. Did he have any interests? She said that he loved airports and would love to work in the baggage area. I suggested she hire an intern from a local college who had dealt with issues similar to her son's and have the intern take her son to work at the airport twice per week. I instructed her to follow these four steps:

1. Find an intern through a local college or hospital.
2. Go to the airport, introduce yourself, and tell them what you want to do.
3. Go to the transitional school and tell them what you plan to do. Ask how they can support your son in this plan.
4. Discuss with the intern your concerns about your son's social skills—how you'd love to see him be able to work and get along with co-workers to the extent possible.

The woman followed the steps, now remotivated at the prospect of her son—regardless of his shortcomings—holding a small job and gaining some independence. She secured a job for her son while in the intern's care for four hours per week. The money he made helped pay for the cost of the intern.

As any child grows, his needs and challenges change. It is important that you stay open to new ideas, programs, and solutions. Don't let complacency or fear compromise your authority. Speaking up, collaborating, and taking charge of your child's future is as important at eighteen years of age as it is at three.

Tips

In the 1998 Disney/Pixar movie *A Bug's Life*, believe it or not the ants teach us at least five strategies for dealing with complacency:

- *Never, ever give up.* Ants never give up. Put something in front of them, and they will get around it, over it, under it, or through it. If one way doesn't work, they will try another. If that way does not work, they will try still another way—and so on until they find a way around the obstacle.
- *Be prepared.* Ants are always getting ready for what's next. They don't ever rest on their laurels. In summer they think about winter and get ready for it.
- *Be industrious and resourceful.* Ants are creatively industrious and resourceful. Ants don't complain about not having the right tools to do what needs to be done. They take what is available in front of them and find a way to make it work.
- *Be optimistic.* Ants are always hopeful. In winter, holed up in their little ant mounds, they use what they stored up all summer. They know that as cold as it is, summer is coming, and they get ready for it.
- *Set your sights high.* Ants don't seem to believe in the concept of enough. They store up all they can for winter. Have you ever seen a restaurant sign that says "AYCE"? I used to think that must be some special brand of food. It took me forever to figure out that it stands for "all you can eat." Instead of focusing on all you can eat, we would do better to focus on what the ants do, AYCD, or all you can do.

If you follow these five tips, you will consistently beat complacency. Think of it as always being hungry to make things better.[11]

Exercises

Fears are feelings we establish when we allow ourselves to recite self-limiting thoughts—like the woman in the example above or myself after my first visit to Friends Academy. On my drive home, my mind raced, reciting all the reasons Friends Academy wouldn't work for Joey. Obsessing about the obstacles made me unmotivated to change. I needed to replace my negative thoughts with positive ones.

The worksheet below will help you affirm your ability to take authority over your child's future. It will help you eliminate self-defeating talk and motivate you to take fresh approaches to alleviating your child's challenges while helping to exemplify your strengths.

Goal-Supporting Worksheet

First, state the short-term and long-term goals you are currently trying to achieve for your child. Example: "Short-term, I want Joey's headaches and nausea to end. Long-term, I want Joey to be in an environment in which he feels socially and emotionally comfortable."

My short-term goal: _____

_____

_____

My long-term goal: _____

_____

_____

Now write down fears that are standing in the way of achieving the goals you noted above. Examples: "Joey has difficulty with transitions." "We can't afford the new school."

Write down supporting statements. Examples: "Sippican Elementary School ends at sixth grade. We would be making the change of schools just a little bit earlier than planned." "I could work additional hours to cover the costs if we didn't qualify for financial aid."

My Fears: _____

_____

_____

_____

_____

My supportive statements: _____

_____

_____

_____

_____

Continue the reinforcement by visualizing your child realizing the goals you wrote down at the beginning of this exercise. Write down what you imagine. Example: "I see Joey sitting at a desk in a horseshoe in his new classroom. He is eating lunch and talking and laughing with his new classmates. He is free of headaches and has begun to make friends."

My visualization: _____

_____

_____

_____

_____

Your focus in this exercise will realign your emotional energy and help you regain your authority. Fears take on many different forms and drain you of energy while robbing you of time you could be using more productively to help your child and yourself. Let your child's developing needs and interests be the motivation to guide you to the best possible outcome.

Step Nine:
DELEGATE

/Delegate/ **To give somebody else the power
to act and make decisions on your behalf**

The playground in Onset—about two towns south of Marion—offers four slides, a bridge, and a jumble of nooks and crannies in which Joey enjoyed enclosing himself. Preferring the seclusion myself, I always looked forward to the days we had time to make the trip. Onset's small winter population—about one-third of its summer residency—left the playground with few visitors during the school year.

I parked the car and noticed three younger children playing on the monkey bars at the opposite end of the playground, their mothers nearby. *Locals*, I thought to myself, having seen them there several times before. Joey headed for his favorite slide as I pulled out a can of Static Guard from the glove compartment. Depending on the temperature of the day, and the material of Joey's clothing, slides often gave off static shocks—a meltdown trigger for Joey. Proud of my preparedness, I retrieved the can and my large mug of cinnamon hazelnut coffee and made my way over. Joey paced back and forth at the top, waiting for me to spray down the slide and fill in a small puddle that had formed in the sandy gravel at the base. With the slide still damp from the morning dew—and no additional supplies in the car—I reluctantly pulled out a gum-infested paper towel from the trash receptacle nearby, wiped the slide down, and sprayed it with a light coating. The puddle presented more of an issue. Water touching Joey or his shoes would mean an abrupt end to our outing. I dumped out my much-needed coffee and began bailing with the cup. All tasks now complete, Joey tentatively sat down and slowly slid to the bottom, keeping his legs spread apart, fearful that remnants of the puddle might still be under the stones. He proceeded back up the stairs to slide down again exactly the way he had climbed up and slid down the time before, a ten-minute ritual at best. My much-needed break had come.

Taking pride in my ability to resolve Joey's issues once again, I brushed off my hands and sat down at one of the four picnic tables. As my eyes took a brief recess from watching him, I noticed that the trio of mothers on the other side had turned their attention to us—disgust, irritation, and disbelief painted on their faces.

"I've heard of spoiled, but come on—dry off the slide?" one of the mothers mumbled.

No one understood. I didn't want—nor did I know where—to begin to explain Joey's issues. I wanted to yell out, "I'm not spoiling him! I'm making the slide tolerable so he can slide down—do everyday things your kids do and you don't have to think about!" At times I secretly wished Joey had Down syndrome or some other visible disorder that people would recognize immediately, thus feeling instant empathy toward him. Rather, Joey was an adorable little boy with blond hair and big brown eyes.

I leaned back, brushed the gravel off my jeans—along with their comments—and closed my eyes, taking peace and comfort in my isolation. I didn't want to be near people who didn't understand.

Two weeks later, with Joey up on the slide and me just finishing the pre-slide prep work, a woman walked over, sat down next to me, and handed me a paper bag. I opened it to find some dish towels, a pail, and a small bar of chocolate. Confused, I asked what it was for.

"I always kept a bag in my car when my oldest son was about your son's age," she said. "I got tired of going through the trash to find something to wipe down the slide. The chocolate bar was my reward after I helped him slide down comfortably."

I had been so alone for so long, I could barely contain myself and began to sob.

Your Exercises

Throughout *Step Ahead of Autism*, we've examined how to minister to the needs of your child. Equally important is the ability to minister to your own needs, something I hadn't done. I had been so focused on protecting Joey from others that I didn't realize how isolated I was—how alone. I didn't know how to begin relying on the help and support of others.

We all need people who know and understand us and our children—people we can delegate some of our responsibilities to, if only on occasion. But delegating is no easy task. After all, you know your child better than anyone else. How can you expect outsiders to know when your child is uncomfortable or anxious if he is unable to communicate his needs?

Turning your child over to any person or situation—babysitters, summer camps, helpful neighbors, birthday parties, grandparents—requires trust. Trusting others outside the school system to care for, understand, listen to, and cooperate with you relative to your child's needs is essential if you are going to delegate and give yourself (and your child) a needed break.

Let's examine why delegating can be so hard:

Reason #1: Isolation Is Easier
A child whose physical appearance to most standards is average to above average, is bright and skillful at many tasks, and has outbursts if things aren't just so can appear spoiled, needy, and immature to family members, friends, neighbors, and strangers. When you explain your child's disorder, many people—perhaps even your partner—question the diagnosis, the required routines, the special attention, and the order that everything needs to occur in for your child to have a smooth day.

The TV show *Parenthood* depicts a married couple with an autistic son, Max. One of the first episodes deals with the reactions of Max's family members when Max's doctors diagnose him with Asperger's syndrome, an autism spectrum disorder characterized by significant difficulties in social interaction, along with restricted and repetitive patterns of behavior and interests. Each family member reacts a little bit differently, from denial and lack of understanding to Max's older sister's disbelief at her parents' shock at the diagnosis.

This range of reactions points out how important it is to have strong support systems in place, not only for autistic children themselves but for their siblings, other immediate or extended family members, and you. Prior to *Step Ahead of Autism*, there was no how-to book for parents, family members, educators, and doctors that addressed the array of reactions you might experience and that provided the strategies, tools, and action plans needed to work through them. The alternative has been isolation. It is easier to isolate yourself and your child from others—family, friends, neighbors, and mothers on a playground—than to explain something you have difficulty accepting yourself, especially when your explanations might be met with disbelief and ridicule.

You quickly learn that trusting others is far too difficult and that isolation is painless and simplistic, an easy coping mechanism. Social isolation comes with its own set of risks, however. As noted by James S. House in "Social Isolation Kills, but How and Why?"[12] the magnitude of risk associated with social isolation is comparable to that of cigarette smoking and other major biomedical and psychosocial risk factors. Isolation can also lead to social loneliness—the loneliness one experiences without a wide social network. You begin to feel like you are not a member of your community; you do not build a circle of friends and allies you can rely on in times of distress.

You can't do it alone, and you don't have to. You need to take the trust you have now developed in yourself and draw on it to trust in others.

Reason #2: Doing It Myself Saves a Lot of Heartache for Me and My Child

I'm sure you've learned that some tasks are done more efficiently alone—whether it's taking out the trash after repeatedly asking your spouse to do it or picking up your daughter's room because you don't want to wait for her to get it done. "Doing it yourself" takes on an entirely different connotation when you're looking after your autistic son or daughter.

You have spent hours, days, weeks, even months exploring what works best, and what doesn't, to help your child just get through the day—the painstaking minutia of every ordinary daily routine: the placement of each and every toy and the timing of when each one will be played with and put back; the rituals before, during, and after going to the bathroom; a full playbill of routines around mealtimes. Then you consider handing over your volumes of information and directives to a babysitter, grandparent, camp counselor, friend, or even your spouse and are expected to trust that this person will follow your lists verbatim when your child is in his or her care. Forget about it—it's just not happening. You would rather do it yourself and understandably so.

In an episode of *Parenthood*, Max's grandfather Zeek takes Max camping overnight. Zeek, still in denial about Max's diagnosis and angered by the excruciating rituals that Kristina, Max's mother, goes through to keep Max from having outbursts, takes all the directions from Kristina relative to Max's routines, knowing full well he has no intention of following them. Kristina, though fearful of letting Max go overnight, figures she can trust her father-in-law to do exactly as she requests and has written down. Zeek, having his own agenda, doesn't follow the routines, leading Max to a traumatic meltdown. The positive occurs when Zeek realizes Max's diagnosis is real. The obvious negative is that Max, Kristina, and Zeek all suffer as the result of Zeek not trusting his daughter-in-law and the doctor's diagnosis. Trust has to be reciprocal. Not only do you have to trust in the people who care for your child, but they have to trust in you and your intentions for your child.

In Step One we talked about trusting your inner feelings and following your intuition. Trusting yourself makes choices easier, lets you express your beliefs, and shifts your feelings from overwhelmed to confident. When you choose to believe that what you are doing for your child is exactly what your child needs—today, right now—you'll begin to experience a greater sense of optimism and confidence, which will lead to others trusting you and the formation of healthy relationships with the people who care for your child. When you build relationships with your child's caregivers—babysitters, family members, camp counselors, even fellow parents on the playground—they will believe and trust in you and respect the choices you've made for your child.

Tips

Following are some factors to consider when delegating responsibility to your child's caregivers:

- *Be open and honest.* Be completely open with your child's caregivers. Honesty should reflect your hopes and desires for your child, but also your fears and concerns. Honesty builds respect. A reciprocal belief in your child's caregivers and their reputations, as well as your own, will lead to open and truthful communication and understanding between you.
- *Don't assume.* Ensure real transparency, clarity, and specifics in all your instructions to your child's caregivers. Never assume anything.
- *Be confidential.* Total confidentially is expected, and all boundaries should be discussed.
- *Manage expectations.* Make sure yours are as clear as possible. Nothing damages trust more than under delivering in any way.
- *Be gentle.* Sensitivity and modesty are key ways to gently build a rapport with your child's caregivers. A parent who comes off as a know-it-all can get on people's nerves.
- *Listen with respect.* Take time to really hear the recommendations your child's caregivers offer. Be open to trying new ideas, and gently point out why a particular suggestion, though a good one, might not be the right fit for your child. Offer to try suggestions that might work at a time when you and the caregiver are both with your child.
- *Be kind.* Demonstrate a genuine care for your relationships. Take the time and effort to develop mutual respect and understanding. Get to know your caregivers on a personal level. Acknowledge their stories—their troubles and joys. Remember it's not all about you and your child.
- *Be confident.* Your ability to deliver all of the above shows a natural self-confidence that will nurture your relationships and will help build trust between you and your child's caregivers.

The next step is to build trust between your child and a caregiver. Explain to the caregiver that working with autistic children can be difficult for a variety of reasons but that many of these challenges can be overcome by gaining your child's trust. The benefits are twofold: not only does your child become more open to working with the caregiver, but bonding and learning provide the caregiver with a much better understanding of your child's personality.

Exercises

Edit the following suggestions to fit your child and use the information to complete "Notes to My Child's Caregiver" on page 104. Ask the caregiver to consider the suggestions to help her gain your child's trust.

Examples

- *Get to know my child's interests.* Many children with autism are incredibly smart and enjoy puzzles and games they can play on their own. Others enjoy small trinkets they can hold onto or keep in their pocket. Ask questions that you would of any other child, such as, "What is your favorite movie?" or "What games do you like to play?"
- *Stay calm and quiet.* A child with autism might become over stimulated quite easily. Sudden loud noises, too much background noise (radio or television), large groups of people, or general chaos can have the child hiding quickly or covering his ears to escape the noise or disturbance. Make sure he knows that if he is ever scared or overwhelmed, he will be safe with you.
- *Sit with him.* Obviously, not all autistic children are the same, but like all children, they sometimes (or often) want to play by themselves. Simply sitting with him while he plays—and not disturbing him—shows you are interested and that you won't break into his comfort zone without permission.
- *Gradually increase interaction.* As my child becomes more comfortable with you, begin to ask questions or make engaging observations, such as, "I see you like the black train. Is that your favorite toy?"
- *Observe physical reactions.* Ask him to hold your hand, give him a hug, or rub his head to see how he reacts to physical contact. He might be perfectly fine with it, or he might become instantly defensive. Don't push this. Also, allow him to hang onto any security items he may have. Many autistic children find comfort in holding onto a particular object throughout the day.[13]

Notes to My Child's Caregiver

My child's interests are: _____

_____

My child needs the following atmosphere to relax: _____

_____

My child will interact best when: _____

_____

My child does not do well when: _____

_____

Other concerns I have: _____

_____

_____

_____

Schedule Caregiver Time

Now that your child's caregiver has an understanding of your child and your expectations, arrange for the caregiver to spend time in your home, playing with your child while you are a room or two away. Set out one of your child's favorite toys and let the caregiver and your child spend one or two hours doing something your child enjoys. Keep an ear open to get an idea of the caregiver's communication with your child and to make sure your child is not unduly stressed.

After the initial encounter, schedule an outing for an afternoon of running familiar errands with the caregiver, with a stop at the playground or the park. The key is to include the caregiver in outings that are familiar to your child while you are present. This will assure your child that the caregiver is familiar with your regular routines while still providing the comfort of your presence. Including a break for fun amid the humdrum of everyday errands gives your child and the caregiver a chance to relate and share some fun away from home. Sit on a bench and enjoy the fresh air while the caregiver pushes your child on the swings. This will help build trust between your child and the caregiver.

In addition, choose more difficult times, such as mealtime or visiting the bathroom, to have the caregiver in your company. The caregiver can be in the background to put your child at ease but within view, so that he or she can see the complexity of your child's rituals and understand the order in which they occur to make these events go smoothly for your child.

After spending as many pockets of time as you deem necessary with your child, under your watchful eye, the caregiver should be ready to babysit for your child while you are not home.

Limit the first unsupervised time with your child to no more than two hours. Do not leave your child with a caregiver for any lengthy period until your child is fully comfortable. Even if your child seems completely thrilled with the caregiver and demonstrates nothing but positive feedback, the tune may change the first time you leave the two of them alone. Adjusting to a caregiver will most likely be difficult for your child. The key is to start slowly. It is not just a matter of you trusting the caregiver and he or she trusting you. Your child needs to trust the caregiver too. Don't rush your child's trust.

It took me close to two months to feel completely comfortable with Joey's caregiver. Two months of open communication, exchanging ideas about what worked best in various scenarios, and leaving Joey's caregiver with him for pockets of time during the week, created a mutual respect and trust. By then Joey's caregiver had formed a supportive relationship with and a strong liking for Joey, which was paramount.

It can be a lengthy process, but having caregivers that you and your child trust (and who trust you) means opening up many positive possibilities for you, your child, and your family.

Step Ten:
ASPIRE

/Aspire/ **To seek to attain or accomplish
a particular goal; ascend, soar**

At six years old, Joey joined the local art center's drama club for grades K–8 to develop an imagination and to learn role-playing skills. Quickly recognizing Joey's rote ability to memorize entire scripts, the director of the art center often gave him leading roles. She once called our house, suggesting he take on longer plays, such as *Peter Pan*, but only if I'd commit Joey to doing it. Joey memorized his lines and everyone else's, correcting them when they went astray. Since he needed to be in control of the world around him, common occurrences such as children forgetting their lines became a source of frustration for Joey, something he couldn't comprehend.

At Friends Academy, drama, art, and music were interwoven into other subject areas. The arts program, a part of his daily routine, allowed Joey to comfortably experience what he had watched for years in Disney movies. The creative multi-arts program tapped the right side of Joey's brain. It slowly, subtly softened his rigid edges.

During the winter of fifth grade, Joey expressed a strong desire to swim competitively. Friends Academy did not have a pool or offer the sport. Joey had taken swimming lessons at Tabor Camp and privately at a

neighbor's pool, but his request to swim on a team came as a major sur-
prise to me. For the first time, Joey came to us and said he was interested
in something, which was reason enough to explore it.

I immediately made phone calls to pool facilities in the area. The New
Bedford YMCA offered boys and girls swim teams, ages five through eighteen. The swimmers competed with kids from other YMCAs in the area, the
teams grouped by age. I made an appointment to meet with Steve Cooper,
head coach of the boys swim team. The scheduling secretary instructed
me to have Joey bring a suit, towel, and water bottle. That Wednesday
afternoon, I picked Joey up from school and drove over to the Y, about ten
minutes away. Joey anxiously flexed his fingers in the backseat.

"We can go another day, honey, if you're tired."

Normally, I'd never suggest a change of plans—a detour in the day—
but taking Joey to try out for a swim team seemed surreal.

"It's today. I want to go today. I'll be fine."

I parked the car, and we headed in. The young women at the front
desk instructed us where to go. Joey changed into his suit in the boys'
locker room, and we headed to the pool area to meet Steve. The thick
and muggy air made it difficult for me to breathe. Focused on the task at
hand, Joey didn't seem to notice. Steve walked over, shook our hands, and
introduced himself. A young guy in his twenties with clean-cut blondish
brown hair, blue eyes, and a slight build, Steve ushered Joey over to the
edge of the pool while I took a seat on the bleachers nearby. Steve con-
cisely instructed Joey on what he wanted him to do.

"Joey, just relax and take a deep breath. Get in dive formation. Then
swim to the end of the pool and back doing freestyle."

Joey dove into the pool—a perfect dive—and swam freestyle as
instructed. Steve then had Joey do the backstroke, the butterfly, and the
breaststroke. Joey performed the strokes precisely and effortlessly. Steve,
clearly pleased with Joey's performance, smiled as he walked over to me
and sat down.

"So Joey's never been on a team before?"

"No."

"And he has never swum competitively?"

"No."

"Where did he learn those strokes? I mean, his technique is flawless—
more accurate than my top swimmers. Are you sure he hasn't?"

"I'm sure," I said, smiling to myself, feeling proud at Steve's amazement. "He learned in summer at Tabor Camp. They give swimming lessons four days a week for about half an hour off their dock. The lessons are basic—treading water, breathing, blowing bubbles, the usual. They don't teach actual strokes like the butterfly, breaststroke, and freestyle."

"Most kids on my team have been swimming competitively since first grade. Joey needs to build his endurance, but his technique is the best I've seen straight out of the gate . . . ever."

Joey could have watched someone swimming on TV and copied exactly what he saw to obtain his technique. I sat quietly, pleased at Joey's apparent success and worried about what this triumph meant—echoing noise; crowded, hot, muggy, and stifling pool areas; the pressure of competition; crowded locker rooms; and long drives to away meets. I so wanted it to work for Joey, but I couldn't comprehend how it would. Steve asked Joey to get out of the pool and walked back over to me. Joey followed him, standing, shivering, and soaking wet, waiting for Steve's next request.

"Joey you can dry off and change your clothes. Your mom and I will meet you at the front desk." Clear, concise instruction again. Maybe this could work. Joey, hanging on Steve's orders, went off into the locker room.

"He's made it on the team. Here's the practice schedule. The meets will be posted next week. We need parent volunteers for timing, snacks, and water."

"Yes . . . sure . . . whatever you need," I said, cutting him off. "Steve . . . Joey is very coachable."

"I can see that."

"No . . . I mean, give him clear, concise directions. He'll do exactly what you want. But you can't be vague and don't assume."

"Okay . . .?"

"I mean, if 'Hit the lockers' means 'Dry off, get dressed, and see you next practice,' tell him that, just once. He won't forget. He's . . . he's very literal."

Seeing my struggle for the right words, Steve put his hand on my shoulder, as if he instinctively knew what I was (and wasn't) saying.

"I haven't had a meltdown yet, not even from one of my five-year-olds . . . and I don't plan on it," he said reassuringly.

My flushed face now burning, I mouthed "Thank-you," afraid that if I spoke the word out loud, tears would escape along with it.

The first weeks of practice went well. Physically exhausted, Joey seemed calmer and less anxious. Then came the first meet against Newport YMCA at home. Swimmers had to be at the pool one-half hour prior to start time, 6:30 a.m. Upon our arrival, I took Joey's hat, coat, and gloves as he made his way into the boys locker room. I entered the pool area, my arms full with Joey's outerwear, unable to find a sliver of space to sit down. At an unbearable 80 degrees, I finally found a corner to unload Joey's gear, wipe off the melted makeup from my chin, and get my bearings. Mothers in tank tops and shorts—their hair neatly clipped back in ponytails or tossed high on top of their heads—sipped Dunkin' Donuts coffee as they bounced around the edges of the pool. *Swim-meet pros*, I thought to myself, as I felt my thick Irish locks implode into a beach ball of frizz. Still in the corner, I peeled off as much clothing as I could, leaving me in a pair of jeans and a long-sleeved fleece shirt.

Leaving my clothes in the corner, I made my way to the pool to try to get some air. Some parents were lined up at either end of the pool with timers and clipboards. Some signed in the swimmers, and others worked at the snack and water table across the hall. I looked for Joey in the maze of skinny boys' bodies dressed in navy blue swimsuits, goggles, and swim caps. Finally spotting him on the swimmers' bleachers, I called his name and waved, but he couldn't hear me over the chatter.

In the pool, six lanes were blocked off with ropes and small buoys. After each group of six swimmers swam in perfect synchronization, six more came off the bleachers, leaving the remaining seated swimmers to move up a row, six at a time. Joey, in the second-to-last row of bleachers, wouldn't swim for a while. I headed out to the snack bar to drop off my donation of Fig Newtons and to retrieve a bottle of water. Sucking it down in two large gulps, I tossed it into the recycle bin and made my way back into the oven. Two hundred parents filled one hundred bleacher seats, with many of us tightly huddled on the sidelines. Many sat on coolers filled with Gatorade, granola, and PowerBars, not allowing other parents to stand in front of them. I couldn't fathom how Joey could handle all this, given that I could barely stand it. I waited in the hallway, checking back in every ten minutes to see where Joey sat in the bleacher chain. When Joey hit the second row, I made my way to find the perfect spectator spot. Parents in the front row dropped back to the last row after their children swam. They had their own synchronization going on.

I positioned myself at the end of the pool where Joey would start and finish. He would swim two laps (up and back two times, I learned) doing freestyle. The swimmers got in their lanes and stood up on the boxes. I felt ill. Someone yelled, "On your mark," and they all bent over into dive position. A coach blew a loud whistle, and off the swimmers went, diving into the pool, splashing the parents in the front row. Covered in pool water, I couldn't take my eyes off Joey long enough to wipe my face.

Everyone screamed, yelled, and cheered so loud that I couldn't hear myself think, but Joey just kept swimming, doing the turns underwater when he came to the edges of the pool and heading back down for the lap. A woman next to me grabbed onto my arm and cheered for her son, who was apparently in first place. Joey turned and headed back down toward me for his final length of the race. Coming to the finish, his fingers reached out and touched the edge of the pool. The whistle blew, and someone yelled out his time.

"Is that your son? He's in second place, second place!" The woman next to me yelled, still vigorously shaking my arm.

I broke free and tried to get through the crowd to congratulate Joey.

Joey pulled off his goggles, asked the timer to repeat his time, got out of the pool, and made his way back to the rotation of the bleachers—and then it hit me. Swimming was Joey. Its starts and stops, its synchronization, its roped-off limits—it was a manageable world for him. He had to rely only on himself. He contributed to a team but laterally, separately, parallel to the other swimmers. It made perfect sense. Focused only on his lane, he didn't hear a single sound except for his time. Swimming competitively was a turning point for Joey. A physically taxing, whole-body sport, it relaxed Joey, leaving little room for anxious moments. And as his endurance increased, so did the respect of his teammates.

As he studied the next three years at Friends Academy, coupled with swimming on a team, Joey's tight, rigid world began to expand. By eighth grade, Joey had begun to lose some of his rote behaviors. His ability to memorize pages of material declined until it reached a level of normalcy. Since the age of five, Joey had had the ability to know what day of the week a date in the future would fall upon. I'd tell him, "Your next doctor's appointment is February 20, 1998," and within seconds and without access to a calendar he'd reply, "Oh, it's on a Tuesday." Now, at age fourteen, predicting the day of the week had become more difficult.

At the same time, he became aware of some of his social inadequacies. He questioned why his younger brother, Mattie, had so many friends, and he wondered how Mattie made friends so easily. Later that year, in early spring, Joey came home one day and repeated a joke that was told at school. I laughed.

"Mom, why are you laughing? I don't get why that's funny. I don't get why anything is funny. I don't get what humor is. I don't get it."

I explained humor to him the best I could. We purchased joke books together and went through them. I explained why each joke was funny and what made it humorous. Joey slowly began telling jokes. Though his presentation was rote, he began to explore a concept that never before existed in his world. It fascinated me that everything—right down to what made him laugh—had to be learned. At the end of eighth grade, Friends Academy held a graduation ceremony in the early afternoon. It was a gorgeous day in early June, the warm air making it feel more like July. Outside in the back gardens, family, friends, and guests of the graduating class were seated in a horseshoe around the graduates' auditorium-style chairs. My mom, now in a wheelchair and ridden with arthritis, sat on the outskirts of the garden with her dear friend and one of Joey's supporters, Mary Coholan. Danny and I—now separated—met at the graduation and sat together. Cherry blossoms from the surrounding trees sprinkled my head each time the warm breeze blew, providing a much-needed diversion from the deafening awkward silence between us.

The school bells rang, bagpipers piped, and we all stood. In walked the graduates single file: the girls in mid-length white dresses, followed by the boys in dark navy blue suits—Joey focused and handsome. We sat down after the graduates took their seats and listened to alumni guest speakers share their successes outside of Friends. Diplomas were handed out individually, while in the corner of the gardens, caterers shuffled in and out, laying down platters of finger sandwiches, salads, and an assortment of desserts. At the end of the ceremony, Claudia Daggett, headmistress, prepared to announce the Head of School Award recipient. Friends Academy grants an award to the student in each graduating class who's most respected by his or her peers and has the highest academic achievement. I gathered my sweater and camera, attempting a quick escape to my mother and friends five rows back. The day had been draining enough without having to explain to other parents why Danny and I had come separately.

"And the award goes to Joseph Burnett."

I froze. Joey had been given the Head of School Award. He stood up, walked over, and shook Claudia Daggett's hand. Everyone rose to their feet and clapped, a few of his fellow students yelling out, "Yay, Joey!" The bagpipers began to play, and one of Joey's teachers, Ms. Rosas, ran over to me.

"You better hurry up and start crying. Otherwise I am going to be the first one." We hugged and cried and cheered as the students walked off through the garden gates.

At the end of the luncheon, Ms. Kelsey came over to me and placed her arm around my waist.

"You knew exactly what you were doing when you placed Joey here, and I commend you. He's a great kid, and you've done a great job."

I thanked her and wheeled my mom to the car, Joey still saying good-bye to his teachers and friends.

High School

Joey's swimming improved dramatically in his last four years at Friends, continually building his confidence and providing a calming outlet. Searching for schools had now changed course; no longer did Joey need special accommodations. Our focus shifted to finding a high school that would foster Joey's emotional strength, self-esteem, and social skills while offering competitive swimming. Bishop Stang High School—located in Dartmouth—was Joey's choice.

Joey had swum outside the YMCA for Southcoast Aquatics, and Dave, the Southcoast Aquatics coach, also coached the boys' swim team at Stang, making the transition easier. And being on a team freshman year would instantly give Joey a group of peers to connect with.

A Catholic school, Bishop Stang required students to wear uniforms and offered a community feel and a nurturing environment. The swim team had a cookout in August before the school year began to go over requirements for being on the team. This event also gave newcomers the opportunity to meet fellow swimmers and upperclassmen.

Joey had signed up for classes the previous spring. Uniforms were fitted and delivered over the summer. We could carpool with local families;

Stang also provided a bus. We opted to drive at the beginning of the year and to work our way into a carpool as the year progressed—once Joey and his schedule were settled.

The first day of school came. I dropped Joey off at 7:20 a.m. and returned back home to get Mattie off to school by 8:35. After I dropped off Mattie, I ran back home to clean up the kitchen. In the midst of doing the dishes, the phone rang.

"Hello?"

"Hi, is this Mrs. Burnett, Joey's mom?"

"Is Joey okay?"

"Yes, yes . . . not an emergency. I'm Sarah Stearns, the school nurse, and I just have a few questions. Do you have a minute?"

"Sure."

"I'm going over Joey's physical form, and his pediatrician has written 'PDD' at the bottom. You know we don't offer a special needs program at Bishop Stang. Is Joey autistic?"

I didn't know what to say.

"Mrs. Burnett? Are you there?"

"No . . . I mean, yes, I'm here. Joey was diagnosed years ago, and he didn't have an IEP at Friends, and he has been doing great since swimming and . . ."

"Mrs. Burnett, is he autistic? Does he have PDD?"

All I could think of as she drilled me was that Joey would be confused and humiliated. Does someone with a disorder understand that they have a disorder? Joey and I had talked about it, and I pointed out instances when the disorder was prevalent, like when he couldn't understand humor or struggled to make friends. When we carpooled to Friends with the neighbors down the street, I'd say, "Mr. Noyes will be here at 7:00 a.m. to pick you up." Joey would pace back and forth anxiously, flexing his fingers if Mr. Noyes arrived one-sixteenth of a second before or after seven. One time Joey complained about it in the car so much that Mr. Noyes pulled to the side of the road and tried to explain estimation to Joey. "Your mom is estimating when she tells you I'll be there at seven. It may not be exactly seven." Joey saw the situation as a flaw in Mr. Noyes, not in himself. Since Joey had been swimming and developing more social skills, some—if not most—of his autistic behaviors had decreased or disappeared. He needed Stang.

The diagnosis of autism is one I never hid behind. Rather I embraced it as a tool, a strategy to obtain the intervention, services, and accommodations Joey needed along the way. He no longer required modifications in the classroom. He needed to grow and develop socially and emotionally. He needed to swim, to learn, to graduate, and to move forward, and I wasn't going to let this thorough school nurse stand in the way of that.

I spent the next twenty minutes stating Joey's case to Ms. Stearns. By the end of the conversation, she seemed satisfied with my dissertation and with Joey's admittance to Stang.

Amy Burke, Joey's beloved babysitter and neighbor since he was young, was a senior at Bishop Stang. Amy had written a reference letter for Joey's application package to Bishop Stang. Hours after our phone call, with his application package in tow, Ms. Stearns called Amy down to her office to learn what else Amy knew about Joey beyond what she had written in his reference letter.

"Joey's an incredible young man," Amy said almost proudly. "I can't believe how far he's come since he was a child—he was so autistic."

Ms. Stearns immediately called me back after Amy left her office, stating that she had had time to rethink our conversation and that she didn't feel Stang was the place for Joey, stating she had confirmed Joey's diagnosis with another member of the Stang community, never revealing to me it was Amy she had spoken with. I slammed down the phone. Here you had a student who was given the Head of School Award for academic achievement, was a contributing member of the swim team, and had received the President's Award for the highest score on the Stang entrance exam, and you are telling me there is no place for him at Stang? I needed someone who loved a good fight and could argue my case like an attorney. I called Joey's dad. Through my gushing whelps and tears, I told him the story.

"I'll take care of it."

About an hour and a half away from the high school, Danny hung up the phone, got in his car, and drove to Bishop Stang. Upon his entrance, he demanded to speak to the principal.

"How dare you deny my son, a boy who passed every piece of qualifying criteria with flying colors, entrance to your school? This is beyond discrimination. Did Joey's mom ever once ask for special arrangements or modifications to his program?

"No."

"So he is being denied entrance at this late date because he has made incredible gains—academically, socially, physically, and emotionally—in his life to this point. That is the reason for his denial? Believe me, nothing would make me feel better than pulling Joey right now, right here today. But Joey wants this, he needs this . . . and you need him. You may not realize that now, but you will. Joey has done amazing things, and he will continue to. We will support him on the outside. We are asking nothing from you except to give him a chance and let him stay."

"I apologize, Mr. Burnett, for making you come all this way. I'll speak to the nurse. Joey's admittance stands accepted."

After Danny called to tell me of his victory and to blow more steam, I went out for a walk. I wondered if this was a sign. Had I done something wrong? Friends and family knew about Joey. I didn't want to hide his diagnosis, but I didn't want it to stand in the way of his progress either. I embraced his diagnosis outwardly, openly, completely when it was in his best interest and kept it in the background when it wasn't.

I had walked about two miles away from my house when my cell phone rang. It was Ellen Burke, Amy's mother. Ellen and I were friends and neighbors. In addition to Amy, Ellen's son Andrew also attended Stang.

"I just wanted to make sure Joey got off okay today."

Immediately, I blurted out what had happened, neither of us knowing that Amy, her daughter, had been questioned by the school nurse.

"I hate this Sarah person," I shouted.

"Anne, I'm so sorry. I can't believe this happened. I feel bad because I raved about Stang to you."

"It's not your fault, Ellen. Sarah stated that she talked to someone, someone I know, who confirmed that Joey was autistic, but she wouldn't reveal the name. Who'd purposely do that?" The two of us tried to figure out what other students from our town attended Stang, but we couldn't come up with anyone.

When we hung up, I cut through the beach and headed up the hill to our house. Halfway up, I saw Ellen's red Ford Windstar coming down the road. She pulled up next to me, Amy crying in the passenger seat.

"It was me," Amy cried. "I thought the school nurse was just making conversation about Joey because he had done so well and everything. I didn't know. I didn't know what she was doing. I love Joey."

"Oh Amy, I know you do," I started to cry. "I'm so sorry you were put in this situation."

"Is he staying?"

"Yes, Danny spoke to them. But Joey doesn't know any of this. Please don't repeat it."

Amy shook her head, signifying that she wouldn't, but she couldn't compose herself. The next day Ellen told me that Amy had cried on and off all night, partly because she felt betrayed by Stang and partly because she felt she had betrayed Joey. That weekend I brought a gift and card to Amy to let her know how much we loved her and how thankful we were that she was in Joey's life.

There were smaller bumps, roadblocks, and detours those four years at Bishop Stang, but I learned how to be a buffer from afar, never once calling upon Stang for help. Despite that first day, Joey proved to be an amazing asset to the school. He was named conference all-star, qualified for state championships in swimming, became valedictorian of his class, and gained acceptance into Brown University. Just as he had chosen to swim competitively, Joey had made Bishop Stang High School his choice. Joey had become his own authority.

Your Exercise

An aspiration is a desire or ambition to achieve. Let your inspirations guide your aspirations. Independence is something we all want for our children, but when a child is autistic, the ability to be independent can seem out of reach. It's difficult to imagine that your child will be able to successfully make decisions for himself.

Be optimistic and focus on the positive gifts your child possesses. Allow each benchmark your child reaches—regardless of how minor—to become a reason for celebration.

Tips

- *Listen.* When your child proclaims she wants to start something new, take time to understand what she wants to do and why.
- *Talk it through.* Talk about the activity with your child.
- *Consider the pros.* Take time to look at the long-range benefits, not just your immediate concerns.

Although I was at first nervous about how Joey would handle being part of a swim team, I considered Joey's love of the sport. In the end, it provided him an opportunity to build his self-confidence and his social and emotional skills.

Exercise

Once each day, week, or month, set an aspiration for yourself in your role as a parent of an autistic child and then break each goal into several steps.

Example
Aspiration: "My goal this month is to have breakfast time be a positive experience for myself and my family."

Steps
1. I will get up a half hour earlier to allow more time at breakfast to help my son get through the meal successfully.
2. I will use paper products to save time on cleanup.
3. I will initially choose only foods my son enjoys eating.
4. I will discuss my intentions with the rest of the family so they can be supportive and helpful.

Define your aspiration: _____

_____

_____

_____

_____

_____

_____

_____

Break each goal into several steps: _____

_____

_____

_____

_____

_____

_____

_____

_____

Measure along the way: Take note of what is and what isn't working. If you find the half hour extra wasn't quite enough, set your alarm for forty minutes earlier rather than thirty.

Reward yourself at benchmarks: Prior to setting your aspiration, note how often your son becomes distressed at breakfast. If you see an improvement, regardless of how slight, reward yourself with something special—a relaxing cup of tea, a walk in nature, a long hot bath.

Putting the Steps into Practice

At the age of fifty-one, and for the first time in a very long time, I became ill. For ten weeks and six different weeklong hospital stays, all by way of an ambulance ride, doctors tried to figure out what was wrong with me. Debilitating aches and pains, no energy, light-headedness, short-ness of breath, bloated stomach, headaches, and high blood pressure were part of a long list of my symptoms. The ordeal frightened me and took a major toll on my family's emotions.

In the eleventh week, by the grace of God, a hematologist questioned whether anyone had performed an Epstein-Barr titer or a mono spot. Mononucleosis is rare in people over forty and unheard of in people over fifty. Because I was fifty-one at the time, the doctors pooh-poohed the hematologist's directive—but I insisted on the test. Having had every other test under the sun in the past ten weeks, from cauterizations to colonosco-pies, a blood test would be by far the least intrusive procedure I'd had in a while. Tests showed a severe case of mono and Epstein-Barr virus. I was probably the first person to hug a hematologist for announcing I had mono.

Having run two marathons and a half marathon in the year prior to becoming ill, one of the first things I wanted to do when I started feeling better was resume my running routine. I had always been a healthy eater and vitamin taker and continued to do so during my recuperation—running would be no problem, I thought. I quickly found, however, I couldn't walk to the end of my driveway without feeling depleted. I struggled for months to run, exasperated at my inability to run five days per week, for a total of at least five miles. One day, I insisted on running four miles with a former running buddy. I ran it well but took a full week to recover. I felt angry and incredibly sad—swearing off running through my tears, as I barely power walked around the block. Then, I remembered a book I fell in love with when Joey was three, entitled *First You Have to Row a Little Boat*, by Richard Bode.

The book talks about how a man, now an avid sailor, first learned to sail. Taken under the wings of a legendary sailor, the author, then a young boy, imagined he would learn to sail on the largest boat in the sea. To his dismay, the sailor instructed him that to learn how to sail, he needed to first learn how to row a little boat. Angered and frustrated that he couldn't just set sail, the boy put off learning to row, wasting time and energy. Eventually the boy, frustrated with his sailing abilities, comes back to the row boat, learns how to row, and realizes the only way to accomplish anything in life is to start at the beginning, breaking down the steps and moving on only when each step is accomplished. Over time, the author steers his way to becoming a legendary sailor himself.

I first learned how to row a little boat when Joey was diagnosed. Breaking down his needs in steps, rolling up my sleeves, putting in the hard work, day-after-day, week-after-week, for months and years, eventually paid off. I decided to lower my sails once again, and start at the beginning as if I had never run before in my life. I didn't start running until I was thirty-nine so I easily recalled the steps I took to start running the first time. Run for five minutes, walk for one, run for five. I broke it down even more and started running every other day, running for four minutes and walking for two. Eventually, I ran three miles without walking or stopping and felt great. The week after that, I ran in my first 5K in three years. Putting in the hard work, taking baby steps, and not looking for a quick fix created a positive outcome for my running and for parenting Joey.

Many parents, when first introduced to the steps, feel overwhelmed at the idea of having to learn yet another avenue to help their child. Parents have said to me, "You sound like a saint," and "You have more time and resources than I do."

In *Step Ahead of Autism*, I left out many details of my life so I could focus on Joey. In some ways, maybe it seems my road was not too difficult. But, like yours, our life was not without other complications and hardships, including life-threatening illness, divorce, another child who was diagnosed with a developmental disorder, and death of family members. Life happens, and most of what we're called to do isn't convenient. I can say with surety, however, that putting in the hard work, time, and effort with your autistic child today, through the practice of the steps in this book, will provide many benefits for you, your child, and your family over the long run.

Tips

Listed here are a few general suggestions to consider when combining the steps and some of the ways I put them to use.

- *Be prepared.* You can't anticipate everything, but you can anticipate many things. The more you can prepare ahead of time, the more resources you'll have to draw upon when faced with a problem.
- *Assess the situation.* When a challenging situation does arise, try to clarify and define the problem as best you can. Don't spend too much time worrying about it. Rather, focus on finding solutions. You can learn to do this by training your mind each time you start worrying to ask these questions:

  a. How severe is it? Is this truly a crisis or merely an inconvenience or a setback?

  b. Does it need to be addressed immediately, or can it wait for an appropriate solution to be developed? The more urgent the situation, the more creative you'll have to be. Be calm and think clearly before taking action.

  c. What is the nature of the problem?

  d. What is really needed?

For example, in Step 5, I chose the Project Grow program in Marion even though it didn't have a summer component. When I assessed the urgency, I realized I didn't need to address the issue of a summer program until later, giving me time to come up with solutions.

- *Assess what is available to you.* Call upon your imagination to use the materials you have on hand at the time.
- *Break the rules.* Don't go around carelessly disregarding the law, but do use things in unconventional ways or go against conventional wisdom or societal norms if it will help. Later in this chapter, in Example #3, you'll see how I applied this tip.
- *Be creative.* Think of crazy possibilities as well as obvious or practical ones. You might find inspiration for a workable solution in one of them.
- *Experiment.* Trial and error may take awhile, but if you have no experience with a particular situation, it's a good way to begin. At the very least, you will learn what does not work.
- *Be decisive.* Once your decision is made, don't analyze; act.
- *Be persistent.* If you go away before the problem does, then you haven't solved anything. Try again, a dozen or a hundred different ways, if that's what it takes. Don't give up. If you don't succeed immediately, that doesn't mean you've failed—consider it *practice*. See the positive in every situation. In Example #2, my persistence pays off.[14]

As you begin to master the steps, your imagination will percolate and ingenious ways to help your child and your family will begin to flow. The five examples below demonstrate ways I applied the steps in combination to benefit Joey and our family.

Example #1: Room at the Inn

Danny and I were married seven years before Joey's birth. One of our favorite places to go, even before marriage, was the Dolphin Inn. Located next to Massachusetts Maritime Academy, the inn has six rooms on the bay, with a small restaurant and bar tucked away. Few people know about this gem except some of the locals and a boater here and there, my dad having been one of them. The dress, as casual as the washboard interior, made me feel comfortable and relaxed, no matter what I had on or how I looked. Walls covered in maritime maps, knots, and tide clocks, give way to the 180-degree view of Buzzards Bay.

We knew Sally, the owner, and one of the waitresses who had worked at the same mortgage company as Danny. Sally lived upstairs and worked downstairs, raising her family along the way. Off the beaten path, a true hidden treasure, the Dolphin Inn was known to attract basketball giants Dave Cowens and John Havlicek, who dropped by to enjoy the piano bar. Pictures of the San Diego Chargers and Boston Celtics sitting at the bar after preseason workouts at the maritime college lined the walls. The atmosphere was homey and simple—I enjoyed it more than any other place except my own home.

After Joey was born, I missed it terribly. I missed the people, yes, but I longed for that comfortable, relaxed feeling again as it now existed nowhere in my life. When Joey turned three, I reminisced and remembered a toddler-size sign in the restaurant with the words "Jason's Paw." Jason, Sally's dog, passed away the year before of old age. The sign remained. Longing to go for an hour or two and knowing Joey's obsession with signs, I made a phone call. After catching up with Sally and sharing the complexities of our situation, I asked if we could come at a time business in the restaurant was slow, so Joey could play with the sign and we could have a drink and relax. Sally, a mother of four, was happy to help.

I packed Goldfish and pretzels for Joey and a small collection of his signs and the three of us headed for the inn. When we got there, the owners had moved the sign to the table in the bar were we had always sat in the past. I felt so moved by their wanting to help and their gratitude at being asked. Joey played for two hours with their sign and the signs I brought with us, stopping now and then for a snack. From this point on, the Dolphin Inn became our weekly getaway.

Steps combined: Trust, Observe, Assess Your Attitude

Example #2: Summer Camp

I provided my own summer program for Joey when he attended Project Grow preschool. When Joey turned seven, I could have sent him to the summer program offered in Middleboro, about thirty minutes away, and his school system would have paid for his tuition, since they did not offer a summer program that ran all day, five days per week. Sippican Elementary School did offer an enrichment program for children grades K–6 three days per week, and children could choose one subject—art, reading, music, or sports. Though I felt the program in Middleboro would be too long of a day for Joey, I felt the summer program at Sippican lacked the structure and activities Joey needed. I checked out the YMCA summer camp offered in the next town over, but the activities were overcrowded and the camp's lack of outdoor shade made it hot and uncomfortable.

Many children in town attended Tabor Summer Camp, a local six-week program that offered a half—or full—day venue. The half day combined three activities, approximately forty-five minutes each, along with a midmorning snack. The oceanside location kept outdoor activities cool. The limited registration kept class sizes small. They offered a multitude of activities, including drama—which Joey was familiar with—and swimming lessons off the dock, leaving no sand for Joey to deal with. It seemed ideal except they didn't offer a special needs program and the attending children—in the confines of the campus—walked from activity to activity unsupervised. Camp counselors were available and scattered about, but Joey would need someone assigned specifically to him.

Being positive, and trusting the caregiver I had chosen for Joey, I went to the camp director and advocated for Joey to attend the camp with his caregiver acting as his aide. Initially, in a phone conversation, the director didn't understand the concept and, having never done it before, quickly dismissed my request. Being persistent, I asked if we could at least meet in person when he had more time to discuss my idea a little further and to see if there were any other options available. I purposely brought Joey's caregiver with me to the meeting. Meeting us in person, hearing my story, and understanding my desire to have Joey attend camp, the director made the necessary arrangements. The program, the activities, the proximity to our home, and the ability to have his trusted aide at his side proved to be the perfect summer scenario for Joey. He returned to Tabor for the following seven years.

Steps combined: Trust, Observe, Advocate, Assess Your Attitude, Delegate

Example #3: The Show Must Go On

When the theatrical production of Disney's *Beauty and the Beast* came to the Wang Center in Boston, I wanted to take Joey. The production was to begin July 2, the day after Joey's eighth birthday. Rather than expose Joey to a traditional birthday party—given his tentativeness around candles and balloons and his anxiety and irritability when people focused on him—taking him to *Beauty and the Beast* seemed the perfect way to celebrate his birthday. I worried, though, about the crowds in the lobby, the long ticket lines, and the ability to clearly see all of the production, especially if we were far away from the stage. I did some research and learned that the Wang Center offers special seating for the hearing impaired. Though Joey's physical hearing was fine, his ability to process what he heard, especially in a crowd, was poor. But getting him into a hearing-impaired seat might be difficult because he didn't fit the theater's criteria, which called for proof that he was diagnosed as being either legally blind or deaf. I talked to Joey's speech therapist, and she agreed to write a detailed letter explaining Joey's deficits. Knowing it would be best if I dealt with someone outside the box office, I called the administrative offices at the Wang Center.

At the time, PDD was not as prevalent as it is today, and I feared that the public relations officer they put me through to might not be familiar with Joey's diagnosis. Armed with my letter from his speech therapist, I decided to make my approach from a hearing-processing, language impaired standpoint. After I explained my situation to the public relations officer, she requested I fax her the letter from Joey's speech therapist along with a copy of his diagnosis, and she would see what she could do. A few days later, I received a call from Wang's box office attendant stating we had four tickets at will call for Saturday's matinee to *Beauty and the Beast . . .* all of them in the hearing-impaired section.

Danny, Joey, Joey's caregiver, and I went to the show. The seats were up close and secluded, housing just the four of us. Joey's caregiver watched over Joey while we retrieved the tickets, snacks, and drinks, keeping waiting times and crowds to a minimum for Joey.

Steps combined: Trust, Advocate, Assess Your Attitude, Ascertain, Delegate, Aspire

Example #4: A Picture Saves a Thousand Meltdowns

Joey's meltdowns occurred when he experienced any abrupt change in plans. His meltdowns were anxiety based and consisted of tears and screams, not violent outbursts. Even so, trying to discuss, discipline, or reason with a child verbally when he is going through a meltdown is difficult at best and can exacerbate the problem.

One of Joey's favorite books was called *Time To*. The star in this picture book was a little boy about six years old. Each page showed the boy doing a different task—time to wake up, time to have your breakfast, and time to brush your teeth. Joey loved the book as he could hear the words and have the visual cue to go along with them. To take it a step further and help Joey with more of his specific tasks, like going to pre-school, I made a book, using pictures of Joey. I took a picture of his back-pack, his lunch box, his classroom, his bedroom, and any place or anything I wanted to put into the book. It worked beautifully and gave Joey a higher level of understanding.

We made many books, around holidays and special events and even about abrupt transitions, such as a fire drill at school. When he would start to get upset, his teacher would hold up that page in the book, and he would understand what was coming.

The books were so successful that I helped other parents make them to get their child through some not so pleasant situations, including aggressive and violent outbursts. Many times during an outburst, an innocent sibling, classmate, or even a parent gets attacked by the distressed child. One book I helped a mom make showed her autistic daughter hitting her younger brother on one page and the little boy crying on the next. When she shared this book with her daughter during a time when her daughter was calm and comfortable, the daughter couldn't believe how she brought her younger brother to tears and felt terrible that she had done so. The mom also showed the events around the meltdown—she had a friend take pictures of her daughter in the throes of a meltdown. We made two versions of the book—one large one for home and a pocket one the mom could carry with her. When her daughter became agitated—heading for a potential aggressive episode—the mom would pull out the book. Her daughter still became agitated, loud, and disruptive, but the physical attacks disappeared. Her daughter understood the outcome.

Steps combined: Observe, Assess Your Attitude, Ascertain

Example #5: A Candle a Day

We've all heard the saying, *An apple a day keeps the doctor away*. In Joey's case, it was a candle a day. Like many autistic children, Joey was highly sensitive and tactile defensive to many things: sand, certain articles of clothing, the slight jolting of the car when I stepped on the brakes, and candles. I recall going to my niece's christening in a large church, the altar twenty yards away. There stood one lit baptismal candle on the altar, barely visible to me. Luckily, it was late spring, and the front door to the church had been latched open. That's where I stood—Joey up in my arms, as far away from the candle as possible so we could avoid a meltdown.

Doctors suggested anxiety medication for Joey, when he was only three. I searched for alternatives. How would he ever learn to deal with these vulnerable feelings?

Ann Stroble at Boston Children's Hospital suggested desensitization. Desensitization is the process of slowly, subtly introducing articles, textures, and events that currently startle your child and leave him feeling anxious—with the goal of helping him learn to be unaffected.

Initially, I began by placing an unlit candle on the kitchen table. The appearance, even unlit, made Joey uneasy, so I started in small segments. First day I left it there for five minutes and the next day ten. At the end of a month, the candle sat on the table like a permanent fixture. Joey would walk through the room—watching the candle's every move—and pass by as quickly as possible. It took two months for Joey to be comfortable with the unlit candle on the table. From there, I started the process of lighting the candle, first for a second, a minute, five minutes—never calling attention to it, making it a natural part of his day.

From there I moved to the car brakes, driving up and down the driveway, with Joey in the back seat, ever so lightly stepping on the brakes. Tolerating the rough texture of sand on his feet came a couple of years later, but worth all the vacuuming and sweeping that came with providing a sandy shore in our home. Desensitization—a lengthy, tedious process to some—was our drug of choice.

Steps combined: Trust, Assess Your Attitude, Ascertain, Aspire

Recently, parked outside of Joey's dorm room waiting to pick him up for spring break, I thought back to all the "will evers" I used to ask: Will Joey ever babble or talk? Will Joey ever eat more than the three foods he eats now? Will Joey ever step out of his routine? Will the meltdowns ever stop? Will Joey ever have friends? Will Joey ever graduate from high school?

Startled by the knock on the window, I jumped out of the car and hugged Joey. I helped him load two months worth of laundry into the back. We got in the car, Joey chatting away about his last six weeks at Brown when I realized I forgot what street to go down next.

"Will you ever find your way home, Mom?" Joey laughed as he gave me directions.

I smiled to myself and thought *I have.* You can too. And you will.

Defining (and Redefining) Success

The March winds blew off Buzzards Bay, leaving traces of salt on my face. I licked my lips as I followed behind Joey to the tire swings, where he signaled me to push him. I pulled back on the chain and pushed Joey forward, my mitten decidedly taking flight alongside. I grabbed the swing, retrieved my glove, and peeled off the chunk of Velcro responsible for its capture. Velcro, now a staple in our home, lined the kitchen and family room walls, making secure holding places for Joey's world. From cup to juice to train to shoe, every item had a picture, every picture had a board—a place—a wall to stick to. Picture cues opened up the language barrier between Joey and me just as they had helped his teachers communicate with him at school. Like most autistic children, Joey needed visuals to help him process what he heard.

According to the American Academy of Pediatrics, children twelve to fifteen months old typically have a wide range of speech sounds in their babbling, begin to imitate and approximate sounds and words modeled by family members, and typically say one or more words (not including mama and dada) spontaneously, with nouns like baby and ball coming first.[15] My expectations for Joey, now two years past these predicated milestones and still nonverbal except for high-pitched shrills, needed to be altered. Selfishly, I wanted him to talk. I wanted to hear the imagined sweet tone of his voice murmur "mama"; to hear the word "up" when he'd stretch his tender arms, gesturing me to hold him; or to see my mom's expression when he called out "Nana" as she made her way to the front door bearing warm casseroles wrapped in hugs. It seemed to me that Joey craved the much-needed outlet of vocalization, his own anxiousness and frustration increasing as he grew physically.

In October we had introduced signing to Joey at his speech therapist's recommendation. Assuming he'd be talking soon, I initially deemed the program a total waste of energy—instead of the blessing it turned out to be. Luckily, I gave in. Once frustrated at trying to get his needs across, Joey now signed his requests. "More," the first sign he learned, miraculously opened up a sliver of his silent world. More juice? Mommy read more? More bubbles? More crackers? Two little hands banging knuckles together, telling me he wanted more and giving me more than he could imagine—allowing me to truly hope that Joey was more intelligent than doctors had suspected. His first speech sounds came in January at three and a half. After weeks of sounds, I raised my expectations and prayed for actual words. The words ball and mama followed—an overdue accomplishment to many, a victory to me. Months later we entered the world of echolalia. Echolalia—repeating heard words or phrases without necessarily understanding them—also can include, as in Joey's case, mimicking the actual tone of voice. The doctors and therapists told me that this stage in Joey's language could last years or longer. They further warned that when the echolalia diminished, Joey might still not understand language.

Joey is speaking words, yes, they explained, but he may never understand what he is saying. Until he begins to demonstrate that he understands what words to say when, and how to use them effectively, he might remain at this level of communication indefinitely.

"Do you want to go on the wooden boat?"

"Do you want to go on the wooden boat?" Joey repeated. We made our way across the playground. I helped Joey climb up a small wooden plank into the boat. I pulled out Joey's signs. He began placing them on the floor, each one in its rehearsed formation.

"Windy today."

"Windy today. Windy today," Joey repeated several times.

As Joey lay on the floor of the boat, thoroughly examining his signs, I sat on the edge of the plank and put my face toward the sun. I thought about the doctor's words and how lucky we were. From pictures to signing to sounds to words—my expectations, redefined along the way, were met each time. Part of me dared not wish for more.

The sun made its initial descent over the merry-go-round, telling me it was time to pack up. I gave Joey the "five more minutes" sign, stood up, and stretched out my legs. Joey's attention now turned to the wheel of the boat. I picked up his signs and tucked them away, curious at his new interest in the wheel, which he continuously spun back and forth. We had been in this boat a thousand times and always followed the same chain of events, the turning of the wheel never one of them. As I turned away to pick up one of the signs, I heard the word "keys" softly spoken. Frightened that I had imagined what I heard, I froze. "Keys." I turned around to find Joey, his eyes focused on me, his stature determined, and his hand palm-side up. "Keys," he said adamantly. Quickly shuffling through my bag, I pulled out my car keys and placed them in Joey's hand. Taking the keys, he placed them underneath the wheel, turned, and made an engine sound: "Brrm, brrm." I dropped everything, ran up the plank, jumped in the boat, and held Joey close, reciting his words over and over: "keys, keys." Crying, laughing, and driving the boat, Joey and I cruised until dark. He had said "keys" and understood what it meant.

Painting a Picture

It would be months after that day at the playground before Joey added new words appropriately—and only here and there—echolalia a continued piece of his repertoire. A year later, echolalia's final departure gave way to a more steady flow of language and understanding. Each time Joey had a small success, a triumph, a victory, I would reassess my expectations. Many experts say that parents of autistic children grieve because "normal" expectations for their children have been crushed and dissolved and might be unattainable. I disagree. I think we are immediately put into a generic pool, given a diagnosis, and told to look at what this means from a larger, broader perspective. We are given the worst-case scenarios, understandably so, and add to those scenarios the volumes of information we find on the Internet and are told by friends and strangers alike.

When Danny and I first decided to adopt children, we were met with caution from family and friends. Their concerns stemmed from the unsuccessful scenarios they had heard about, seen on television, and read in books and magazines. My brother Bob, having worked for the Massachusetts Department of Social Services for more than twenty years, fell witness to unspeakable acts performed in foster care homes and by indigent birth parents. When he and his wife were faced with infertility issues, they never considered adoption.

Had we based our potential success in adopting a baby on my brother's work experiences or others' concerns, we would have failed before we started. We needed to take the broad strokes that had been painted for us and break them down into stages, compartments, and pieces and then celebrate the small successes along the way:

- Making our decision to adopt
- Finding an agency we felt comfortable with
- Getting our home and finances in order
- Having a home study performed
- Being put on the waiting list
- Staying optimistic while on the list
- Being matched to a birth family
- Making sure all legalities were met
- Bringing home our child

The wait—more than four years from the time we began the adoption process to Joey's homecoming—at times seemed unbearable. The wait for Mattie, our younger son, was just as long. Yet the years melted away the minute they were placed in my arms. I can't imagine my life without them. I'm thankful every day that I approached the adoption process with the positive, optimistic attitude it deserves and celebrated the small successes along the way rather than yielding to the broad strokes that had been painted for me.

Our barometer for the success of our children is largely imposed by external influences such as the medical field, family members, our children's peers, parent guides and baby books, and our egos. We tend to be driven by what we have been exposed to—what we've been taught to expect. Our egos suggest that we are entitled to the attainment of society's definition of success and should expect nothing less. Society's definition of successfully attaining language—and the American Academy of Pediatrics' definition of reaching verbal milestones—didn't work for Joey. Did that mean he wasn't successful? No, it meant that I needed to change my definition of success for Joey and to attain a different set of milestones, not a lesser set.

Seasoned parents know this to be true, whether their child is developmentally challenged or not. Breaking down the school years, the milestones, the disappointments, and the achievements helps them and their children focus on what is in front of them today, here and now, not on what is yet to come or what has gone by.

Recently, while checking out at the grocery store, a young pregnant woman waited on me. I asked when she was due. "Two weeks." She told me she knew she was having a little girl, and she feared she would be a worrier like her mother. She even expressed concern about the day her unborn daughter got her driver's license.

I smiled and said, "You have plenty of time to worry about that." As I loaded my trunk with groceries, I thought about the store clerk's comment and the broad strokes she had painted in her mind during her pregnancy. I thought about all the worries, wonders, joys, disappointments, and victories this young woman and her daughter would experience well before her daughter is old enough to drive. A parent is not going to worry when a child is in preschool about whether he or she will have a date for the prom; it is too broad of a stroke, too abstract. Yet we make a similar leap when we first hear our child's diagnosis.

Remember to determine your own gauge for success. Take stock of the little things that your child has achieved and continue to revisit your gauge, reassessing your goals along the way.

Joey ended up being high functioning, yes, but when first diagnosed, Joey started out exactly like any other autistic child. He had no form of speech except for frustrated, high-pitched squeals. He flapped his arms, swung in his chair for hours, slept and ate poorly, didn't like to snuggle, and easily startled. He was tactile defensive, obsessed about certain toys, and hated candles, car brakes, sand, smells, noise, being touched, and the list went on. Dr. Brazelton and his team recommended that Joey attend the May Institute, a year-round, residential-only program for acutely autistic and mentally challenged children.

A Psychologist's Viewpoint

There are many ways we define our children's success and our success as parents. Academic achievements—a high GPA, being on the honor roll, acceptance to the best colleges—are almost universally accepted symbols of success. Income is another. Yet many other dimensions can readily be seen as success. Yesterday I shared some good laughs with my aunt, even though she was terribly sick. Then I watched a fascinating movie on TV. And I'm in a great mood today. These accomplishments are unrelated to my income, academic achievements, cognitive level, or social standing. They are not what we generally think of when we think of success. Yet these accomplishments—these sorts of experiences—make my life interesting and meaningful.

You want your child to be happy, to be a nice person, to be loving, to accomplish "things"—whatever they might be—to give back to the community in some way. You want your child to enjoy interests, have passions, feel empowered, and experience a sense of well-being. When you come to recognize the great value of these experiences, success becomes less linear and one dimensional and more textured and related to quality of life rather than quantifiable achievements.

I had initially hesitated to become involved in this book, even though Joey and his mother have been an inspiration to me. I felt concerned that other parents might either: a) become discouraged if Joey's outcome far exceeded their own child's in terms of so many measures of success, or b) believe that if they did just as Joey's mother had, they would have a similar amazing outcome, even though we know that with this very variable diagnosis, there is no "magic formula" guaranteeing a specific outcome.

However, as Joey's mother and I communicated more about this concern, I realized that the details of one family's journey, in the context of universal processes—the steps outlined throughout the book, steps that apply regardless of a specific child's characteristics or course of development—could help many people, despite differences in their particular situations.

Daniel Gilbert, in his book *Stumbling on Happiness* (Vintage, 2007), writes that "just as memory plays tricks on us when we try to look backward in time, so does imagination play tricks when we try to look forward." He points out, in a wonderful integration of research and common sense, that we meet the imagined future not as our current Self but as a future, changed Self, a person who is also changed in ways we can't imagine.

Having a child with autism changes one's perspectives in so many tangible and subtle ways, and differently for each person, differently over time. Parents of a newly diagnosed child can find it difficult to imagine how the child might be happy or successful if he doesn't achieve certain milestones. You might not be able to imagine being happy unless your child is able to go to college, get married, have a job, speak, have a group of friends, or live independently. I know many individuals who live happy, meaningful lives, and whose parents do as well, who haven't achieved some or all of these goals. This is not to deny the very real grief most parents naturally go through in learning their child may have fewer skills and choices in life compared with what they had anticipated. Yet as humans we have a remarkable ability to adapt to our ever-changing reality and to find joys and successes to celebrate.

Karen Levine, PhD
Instructor, Harvard Medical School
Cofounder and Codirector, Autism Program,
Boston Children's Hospital;
Cofounder and Codirector,
Autism Center, Cambridge Health Alliance;
Recipient, 2010 Federation for Children with Special Needs
Founders Award

Hard work, perseverance, acceptance, optimism, and above all wanting Joey to be happy and to feel loved were the ingredients for our success, as we defined it. When Joey became valedictorian, it gave me the same level of joy as when he said the word keys. His acceptance into Brown was equal to my discovering how touching street signs brought Joey comfort when we'd go for a walk. Parents who have never been blessed with the joy of raising an autistic child might not believe these statements or understand them.

Quantum physics suggests that if you change the way you look at things, the things you look at change. Research shows that at the tiniest subatomic level, the actual act of observing a particle changes the particle. The way we observe these infinitely small building blocks of life is a determining factor in what they ultimately become. If we extend this metaphor to larger and larger particles and begin to see ourselves as particles in a larger body called humanity or—even larger—life itself, then it's not such a huge stretch to imagine that the way we observe the world we live in affects that world.

Think of this little journey into quantum physics as a metaphor for you and your child's life. Your feelings of success depend on your positive view of yourself, your child, your life, and the universe from which success is realized. Changing the way you look at things is an extremely powerful tool. Start by examining how you look at things. Is the universe matching your way of looking and responding in kind?

These pages offer no magic diet or fairy-tale pill. I am not a warrior mom. Success is subjective, meaning different things for each one of us. Not knowing how you define success in your child's life can make the process of your child feeling successful even more challenging. Be clear and definitive about your definition of success for your child. Be thankful and filled with awe and appreciation for each and every triumph along the way. View your world as one that provides rather than restricts. Trust your instinct, follow your heart, and love your child for all the gifts he brings. Change the way you see things, and the things you see will change.

Your Next Steps

Recently I attended the funeral of my dear friend's father, Kenny, who passed away at age ninety-two. I have known Chrissie, Kenny's daughter, since kindergarten, and though we saw less and less of each other over the years, when we did meet at a graduation, a wedding, or a funeral, we would easily pick up where we had left off. Attending the funeral made me a little anxious, as a lot had changed since I had last seen Chrissie, her family, and our close grade school friends.

I planned to go to the church and to stay for a brief moment afterward to pay my respects. But Chrissie's family had planned a luncheon. Two and a half hours later, after talking nonstop, Chrissie, our old classmates, and I—the last ones to leave—hugged and promised we'd get together more often. Driving home I noticed how rejuvenated and refreshed I felt, completely at peace with myself and my life. I realized that talking for those two-plus hours—about our old endeavors and common interests—had revitalized me. I was with a group of people who shared a common history, memories, and past events that no one else could fully appreciate. The round table at that luncheon had all the makings of a "group": We were all close in age, shared a history, and had common interests.

When people come together as a group with more than one commonality, a power, enlightenment, and strength that is inspiring and soothing to the soul emerges. By joining with others in supporting your autistic children, you'll find strength, comfort, joy, and encouragement.

While I traveled most of my path on my own, that isn't necessary or optimal. Members of support groups share experiences and advice. It can be helpful just talking with other people who are in the same boat. You might not be drawn to support beyond that offered by family and friends. Maybe you're not a "group-joining" person, or you might not feel you have the time to spare. But being with a group of like-minded people who are going through the same experiences offers a power you can know only if you experience it. If you think it might be helpful to turn to others outside your immediate circle, joining an autism support group can help you cope better and feel less isolated. You'll make connections with others facing similar challenges. Several organizations hold autism support group meetings, and I have listed those that do in the resource section.

Implementing the Step Ahead of Autism Support System

A Step Ahead of Autism support system or group helps parents implement this book's strategies and tools into their daily lives and provides a platform for doing this with like-minded parents facing similar obstacles. The power of building a community based not on denial or defeat but on trusting and sharing more of yourself as a parent, to benefit both you and your child, will prove to be immeasurable.

You can use the steps in this book several ways. If you are already part of a support group, *Step Ahead of Autism* can be used as the basis for meetings, with group members focusing on one step each week or month. You can also participate in a teleseminar with me, create or join an existing Step Ahead of Autism group, or host a virtual Step Ahead of Autism group via Facebook, Google, or my Web site, www.alleviateautism.com.

I offer a teleseminar for parents, grandparents, and teachers of children diagnosed with autism. Following the steps in this book, the sessions bring you the latest learning, understanding, and approaches, so you can be the parent your child needs—supportive, challenging, advocating, positive, passionate, and certain.

If you are currently a member of 1 of the 150 support chapter groups offered by the Autism Society, consider bringing this book to your meetings and doing the steps together. Group members can determine the directive of each week's meeting, either following the sequence in *Step Ahead of Autism* or taking the steps out of order to focus on what the majority of the group wants to concentrate on.

Who Can Join a Step Ahead of Autism Group?

Mothers, fathers, grandparents, and siblings of an autistic child can join or start a Step Ahead of Autism group. Teachers, day care workers, teaching assistants, and caregivers are also welcome to start or join a group or to take one of my workshops or my teleseminars.

From there, the focus of the group, or more specifically the order in which the steps are taken, examined, and practiced, will be based on the situations of the participants. You will more than likely have a cross section of participants: those whose children have been newly diagnosed, seasoned parents, and those concerned about their child's behavior but with no determination made at that point.

For the latter group, you could start with Step 2, "Observe," and follow the exercises. You could guide each other through observing your children, noting your observations, and providing complete reports for your pediatrician. From there you could work through the diagnosis process and move on to the other chapters, beginning with Step 3, "Accept." It might be beneficial to have seasoned parents work with parents of newly diagnosed children through the acceptance process—focusing initially on areas you have accepted in your and your child's life and moving forward together as a cohesive group through those areas you are struggling to accept.

Seasoned parents might want to move directly to Step 6, "Advocate," brush up on their advocating skills and on learning to work more collaboratively with their child's educators.

Step Ahead of Autism groups can consist of a primary group of mothers, fathers, and relatives and might have subgroups of educators, babysitters, and neighbors. Within those groups, you will have varied profiles: concerned, newly diagnosed, and seasoned.

Starting a Step Ahead of Autism Group

Starting a Step Ahead of Autism group can be fun, empowering, and informative. One mother I spoke to went to libraries in her town and neighboring towns. She posted flyers stating that she wanted to start a group around a book she had read and wanted to share with parents and relatives of autistic children. She held the first "book club" meeting at a local library, where she introduced a draft copy of *Step Ahead of Autism*. The participants signed up, obtained their own draft copies, and planned to meet one month later to discuss the book. She held the second meeting at her home in a relaxed setting, with food and drink. Members discussed the book, and when they came to the discussion about the value of joining a group, the woman announced her intention to start a Step Ahead of Autism group to work through the steps in the book. More than two-thirds of the participants signed up. They meet monthly and take turns holding two-hour meetings at one another's homes. They structure their meetings as follows:

- Twenty minutes for catching up and socializing
- Twenty minutes for reviewing items from the previous meeting
- Twenty minutes for administrative items, announcing local events, and introducing new members
- Sixty minutes working through a step in the book

You can start a Step Ahead of Autism group through an Autism Society chapter group, a local play group, a parent–teacher organization, or a church group. You can also post notices on your child's school Web site or in pediatric offices, day cares, hospitals, libraries, or grocery stores—anywhere parents might venture.

If you don't have time to start a Step Ahead of Autism group but would like to belong to one, or if you want one-on-one instruction in the privacy of your home, go to www.alleviateautism.com. Under the "Get Empowered" tab, click on "Discovery Workshops" and join me for an overview of my teleseminars. In this valuable free seminar, I offer a solid, experience-based approach to dealing with your child and the many challenges you face. This is a great way to get started and offers a convenient avenue to work on the steps with other parents, under the direction of someone who has been through the steps and helped other parents work through them. I personally facilitate all teleseminars and in-person classes through www.alleviateautism.com.

A Step Ahead of Autism group can be as small as two members or as large as fifty or more. Large groups benefit most by breaking into subgroups. In forming your Step Ahead of Autism group, consider the following:

- Number of members
- Location of meetings
- Time of meetings
- Regularity of meetings

You will also want to collect the following:

- Profiles of members
- Members' vision statements for themselves and their children

These actions do not have to take place at the first or even second meeting but should occur early in the development stages. After that, it is easy to set up the agenda for each meeting using *Step Ahead of Autism* as your guide. You might want to designate a member as the facilitator of the group. The facilitator can lead members through the steps and assign "homework," having members map out and break down their vision statements into smaller goals and apply the steps to achieve them. As goals are achieved, members can share their previous month's successes and how the steps helped them.

Each individual brings a unique perspective to raising an autistic child. Everyone's educational background, upbringing, and professional experience are different, as is everyone's approach to dealing with autism. When it comes time to tackle a difficult issue, there is a distinct advantage in having multiple unique perspectives. Some group members might see a solution where others do not. Once a step has been introduced, the group can work on a unified process through the exercises, moving each other, and their children, toward a more positive outcome.

Joey's Valedictorian Speech

June 1, 2008

I would first like to extend my salutations to His Excellency Bishop Coleman, Superintendent Milot, members of the school administration, clergy, faculty, family, friends, and most especially the class of 2008.

I have learned so much at this school—both in and out of the class-room. I would like to share with you all three things I have learned while at Bishop Stang.

First, I learned that, even in seemingly barren situations, friends are always nearby. Does everybody remember what they thought as they walked into freshman lockup? I can still remember I had a swim meet at the YMCA that afternoon and wasn't too pleased to be locked up in the gym with a bunch of people I still barely knew. I didn't feel like shifting gears and wasn't sold on the idea of being around people I didn't know.

However, when I walked into the gym, I was transformed . . . it was a much unexpected experience of getting to know each other. I remem-ber I got so much out of lockup, especially a stomachache from eat-ing too much food, a teardrop or two on my palanca letters, and most importantly better knowledge of a group of people in my class and renewed faith in God. I got so much support from that experience, even when I thought there was nothing. Friends in seemingly barren places has even been a theme in many of our English classes (anybody remember

The Bean Trees?). I thought it was extremely important to know that, and I hope you will always take that with you, Class of 2008.

Second, I have learned that virtue and faith indeed grow in the face of adversity. I would like to quote the wisdom of Ovid, an ancient Roman poet. Ovid once said, "*Crescit sub pondere virtus,*" which translates to, "Virtue grows in adversity." At one time or another, each of us has experienced some form of adversity, or difficulties, or times when things just don't go right. Over the years, each of us has contributed to our class in ways that only two hundred or so unique individuals could. I can confidently say that each of us has changed since we first entered the front doors on that rainy day in August 2004. We each have overcome our own challenges and trials and have been molded by those trials into the young men and women we are today. But look at what we have worked together to overcome! We have made our voices heard, a light shining in the metaphorical darkness of our society. As a Catholic school, we have stood by each other and built each other's faith in God. Furthermore, from that faith we have branched out to aid others in need. It may have been difficult at times to sacrifice our own possessions for others, but we have become better people through those sacrifices. I think that is truly admirable, for what is life if we cannot share our own bounty with others? Together, we have grown in virtue and in faith.

Finally, and most importantly, I learned that, no matter what, you should always follow your heart. This is what helped me to arrive at the first two lessons. At freshman lockup, I remember just letting my heart let go of my past inhibitions and sing "Big, Big House," complete with hand motions. It also helped me to evolve over the course of the past four years. If you haven't already, I'm sure that all of you will arrive at a significant crossroads somewhere in your life. No matter how much you cross-analyze and fragment a situation, the only question remaining will be, "What is your heart telling you?" Each of you will have that gut instinct to follow when the time comes . . . I urge you to follow it.

I'd like to leave you all with one final thought. Our world is changing rapidly, and our greatest challenge is to keep up with its pace. If you keep in mind that there will always be support through the difficult times, and that your heart will guide you, I'm sure you will find happiness. Class of 2008, we *are* the future! We are only limited by our dreams, so let's dream big! God bless and good luck in all of your future endeavors.

❧ Resources

Alleviate Autism
Alleviate Autism provides you with the tools and guidance you need to be proactive with your child's educators, doctors, family members, and friends, and in every other area of your child's life. You can sign up for a free preview event, an eight-week tele-seminar series, or a workshop in your area.
Go to their Web site to find a support group in your area.
http://www.alleviateautism.com

Autism Society
The Autism Society works to improve the lives of all affected by autism through education, advocacy, services, research, and support.
Go to their Web site to find a support group in your area.
http://www.autism-society.org

Autism Speaks
Autism Speaks has grown into the nation's largest autism science and advocacy organization, dedicated to funding research into the causes and prevention of, treatments for, and cure for autism; increasing awareness of autism spectrum disorders; and advocating for the needs of individuals with autism and their families.
http://www.autismspeaks.org

Autism Organizations—Worldwide
The World Autism Awareness Day resolution encourages all Member States to take measures to raise awareness about autism throughout society and to encourage early diagnosis and early intervention.
http://www.worldautismawarenessday.org

❧ Notes

Foreword
1. "Autism Spectrum Disorders," Centers for Disease Control and Prevention, accessed March 2010, http://www.cdc.gov/ncbddd/autism/data.html.

Preface
2. "Autism Developmental Disabilities Monitoring Network," Centers for Disease Control and Prevention, accessed March 2010, http://www.cdc.gov/ncbddd/autism/documents/AutismCommunityReport.pdf.

Step Ahead to a Better Outcome
3. "Facts and Statistics," Autism Society, accessed March 2010, http://www.autism-society.org/about-autism/facts-and-statistics.html.

Chapter 2

4. "Facts and Statistics," Autism Society, accessed March 2010, http://www.autism-society.org/about-autism/facts-and-statistics.html.
5. "Autism Overview: What We Know, National Institute of Child Health and Development, accessed March 2010, http://www.nichd.nih.gov/publications/pubs/upload/autism_overview_2005.pdf.
6. "About Autism," Autism Society, accessed March 2010, http://www.autism-society.org/about-autism.
7. While this is the author's list, many of the items and the initial idea came from two sources: "Sensory Processing Disorder Checklist: Signs and Symptoms of Dysfunction, Sensory Processing Disorder Resource Center, accessed March 2010, http://www.sensory-processing-disorder.com/sensory-processing-disorder-checklist.html, National Institute of Child Health and Human Development, accessed March 2010, http://www.nichd.nih.gov/publications/pubs/upload/autism_overview_2005.pdf-Checklist.

Chapter 5

8. I have used Michael O'Connor's work as a springboard for these exercises. O'Connor, coauthor of *The Platinum Rule* (Warner Books, 1996), identifies six characteristics of flexibility, which is one of the two components of adaptability. "Do You Have Adaptability," Success magazine, accessed March 2010, http://www.success-magazine.com/Do-You-Have-Adaptability/PARAMS/article/256/channel/21.

Chapter 6

9. "Building the Legacy: IDEA 2004," U.S. Department of Education, accessed March 2010, http://idea.ed.gov.
10. "Helping Children with Autism," Helpguide, accessed March 2010, http://www.helpguide.org/mental/autism_help.htm.

Chapter 8

11. "Motivation: The Cure for Complacency," Boxing Scene, accessed March 2010, http://www.boxingscene.com/motivation/56783.php.

Chapter 9

12. James S. House, "Social Isolation Kills, but How and Why?" Psychosomatic Medicine 63, no. 2 (2001): 273–274, http://www.psychosomaticmedicine.org/cgi/content/full/63/2/273.
13. "Teens: Expert Answers On," Children's Physician Network, accessed March 2010, http://kidshealth.org/PageManager.jsp?dn=cpnonline&lic=142&cat_id=20646&article_set=60500&tracking=T_RelatedArticle.

Chapter 11

14. "How to Be Resourceful," wikiHow, accessed March 2010, http://www.wikihow.com/Be-Resourceful

Chapter 12

15. "Developmental Milestones: 12 Months," American Academy of Pediatrics, accessed March 2010, http://www.healthychildren.org/english/ages-stages/baby/pages/Developmental-Milestones-12-Months.aspx.

🙰 Index

About the Author

Anne Moore Burnett has twenty years' experience successfully raising an autistic child. Educators, doctors, psychologists, and counselors have referred hundreds of parents to her over the past eighteen years for direction and advice in the field of autism. The founder of Alleviate Autism (www.alleviateautism.com), she provides workshops, teleseminars, and one-on-one consultation for parents, family members, and anyone touched by autism. For more information, e-mail anne@alleviateautism. com. (Photo © Bodil B. Perkins, Unique Photographs by Bodil)

Also Available from Sunrise River Press

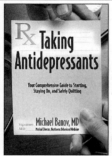

Answers to Anorexia
A Breakthrough Nutritional Treatment That Is Saving Lives

James M. Greenblatt, MD This new medical treatment plan for anorexia nervosa is based on cutting-edge research on nutritional deficiencies and the use of a simple but revolutionary brain test that can help psychiatrists select the best medication for an individual. Anorexia is a complex disorder with genetic, biological, psychological, and cultural contributing factors; it is not primarily a psychiatric illness as has been believed for so long. Dr. Greenblatt has helped many patients with anorexia recover simply by correcting specific nutritional deficiencies, and here he explains which nutrients must be supplemented as part of treatment. He finally offers patients and their families new hope for successful treatment of this serious, frustrating, and enigmatic illness. Softbound, 6 x 9 inches, 288 pages. Item # SRP607

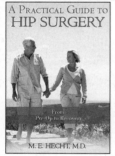

Taking Antidepressants
Your Comprehensive Guide to Starting, Staying On, and Safely Quitting

Michael Banov, MD Antidepressants are the most commonly prescribed class of medications in this country. Yet, consumers have few available resources to educate them about starting and stopping antidepressants. Dr. Michael Banov walks the reader through a personalized process to help them make the right choice about starting antidepressants, staying on antidepressants, and stopping antidepressants. Readers will learn how antidepressant medications work, what they may experience while taking them, and will learn how to manage side effects or any residual or returning depression symptoms. Softbound, 6 x 9 inches, 304 pages. Item # SRP606

A Practical Guide to Hip Surgery
From Pre-Op to Recovery

M.E. Hecht, MD This book tells you everything you need to know before you undergo hip replacement or resurfacing surgery, directly from an orthopedic surgeon who has performed countless hip surgeries and has undergone a double hip replacement herself! Dr. M.E. Hecht tells you step by step what you'll need to do before the day of your surgery, and then walks you through the procedure itself so that you know exactly what to expect. Sharing from her own experience as a hip surgery patient, she also discusses issues that can arise during the first few days through first months of your recovery, and includes handy checklists to help you organize and plan for your post-surgery weeks so you can focus on recovering as quickly and smoothly as possible. This book is a must-read before you undergo surgery, and will prove to be a trusted and essential resource during and after your hospital stay. Softbound, 6 x 9 inches, 160 pages. Item # SRP612

Manage Your Depression through Exercise
The Motivation You Need to Start and Maintain an Exercise Program

Jane Baxter, PhD Research has proven that exercise helps to lessen or even reverse symptoms of depression. Most depressed readers already know they need to exercise, but many can't muster the energy or motivation to take action. *Manage Your Depression through Exercise* is the only book on the market that meets depressed readers where they are at emotionally, physically, and spiritually and takes them from the difficult first step of getting started toward a brighter future. Through the Move & Smile Five-Week Activity Plan, the Challenge & Correct Formula to end negative self-talk, and words of encouragement, author Jane Baxter uses facts, inspiration, compassion, and honesty to help readers get beyond feelings of inertia one step at a time. Includes reproducible charts, activities list, positive inner-dialogue comebacks, and photos illustrating various exercises. Softbound, 6 x 9 inches, 192 pages. Item # SRP624